creative ESSENTIALS

HELEN JACEY & CRAIG BATTY

WRITING AND SELLING
ROMANTIC COMEDY
SCREENPLAYS

creative ESSENTIALS

First published in 2014 by Kamera Books,
an imprint of Oldcastle Books,
PO Box 394, Harpenden, Herts, AL5 1XJ
www.kamerabooks.com

Copyright © Helen Jacey & Craig Batty 2014
Series Editor: Hannah Patterson
Editor: Anne Hudson

The right of Helen Jacey & Craig Batty to be identified as the authors of this work has
been asserted in accordance with the Copyright, Designs and Patents Act 1988.

All rights reserved. No part of this book may be reproduced, stored
in or introduced into a retrieval system, or transmitted, in any form
or by any means (electronic, mechanical, photocopying, recording or
otherwise) without the written permission of the publishers.

Any person who does any unauthorised act in relation to this publication
may be liable to criminal prosecution and civil claims for damages.

A CIP catalogue record for this book is available from the British Library.

978-1-84344-110-6   (Print)
978-1-84344-111-3   (epub)
978-1-84344-112-0   (kindle)
978-S-84344-113-7   (pdf)

Typeset by Elsa Mathern in Franklin Gothic 9 pt
Printed and bound by CPI Group (UK) Ltd, Croydon, CRO 4YY

ACKNOWLEDGEMENTS

The following people and places were invaluable in helping this book happen. Firstly, thanks to our publisher, Kamera Books, and in particular Hannah Patterson and Ion Mills – for sharing our vision and for their patience! And thanks to Anne Hudson, for doing a great job with editing.

We're very grateful to Bournemouth University's Fusion Fund for supporting travel and research to Australia and the US, which was also invaluable for reducing the number of late-night Skype sessions during the evolution of this book. And to RMIT University for its generous acknowledgement of the time needed to research and write.

Special thanks go to Linda Seger, who introduced us in the first place at Carluccio's restaurant in London – a great place for a chumcom meet cute!

Thanks also to Hal Ackerman, Ben Cookson, Julian Farino, Gene Wayne Hart, Andy Horton, Suya Lee, Jeff Reno and Stayci Taylor for sharing their time, insights and thoughts about all things romcom.

Huge thanks to Jule Selbo for agreeing to write the Foreword – we couldn't have a better screenwriting genre expert on hand!

We'd also like to thank our families, friends, students, colleagues and collaborators for helping to make this book happen. Together, they've offered us moral support and guidance, inspiration and reflection, and knowledge that has influenced and transformed our thinking about romantic comedy screenplays and how to talk to others about them.

CONTENTS

FOREWORD

Dr Jule Selbo, award-winning screenwriter and Head of the MFA in Screenwriting at California State University, Fullerton

I began teaching film genre for screenwriters seminars a few years ago, and when I get to the romance and romantic comedy genres, I never tire of asking the writers in the class – *Who believes in true love?* Hands go up – and, surprisingly, more male hands than female hands. We talk about why the idea of true love is a staple in most cultures and societies, and how this idea of a 'soulmate' is so prevalent in reams of literature and films. We discuss possible reasons for why the romance genre is a dominant or supporting story element in many screenplays – top action/thriller/crime films such as the *Bourne* cycle and *The Departed*, westerns such as *Tombstone*, horror films such as *Let the Right One In*, fantasy/war/ sci-fi adventure films such as *Avatar*, and countless more films in various genres.

What makes *Die Hard*, often considered one of the top action/ thrillers, work so well? Because John McClane's <u>reason</u> to enter the fray is to save his wife, so he has the opportunity to rekindle their relationship. He <u>loves</u> her. And that makes us love him. One of the most important elements about the *James Bond* re-boot is that audiences watching *Casino Royale* become emotionally attached to a man who almost gave up the spy game for <u>love</u>. His 'soulmate', Vesper Lynd, dies tragically in the narrative, and now Bond is a haunted, hurting man – albeit still looking great in a tuxedo. We know he's known and given profound, gut-wrenching love. And we love him for that. Audiences tend to love lovers. Because we know how much love can 'hurt', how love can lift a person, how love can cause crises of self-esteem, how it can make or break one's day – basically how it affects us and affects a great majority of (all?) people all around the world.

Film theorist Torben Grodal suggests that humans are connected to the idea of love because of a deep-seated human desire for intimate connection, whether it's for survival, for procreation, for status or for self-esteem. Grodal also refers to Nico Frijda's work, *The Emotions*, positing that <u>true love</u> often comes with a <u>negotiation</u> between partners – what's acceptable, what's not, how far one's willing to go and how much one's willing to risk.

Anthropologist and human behaviour researcher Helen Fisher, in her TED talk, *The Brain in Love*, points to the activity in the brain in the ventral tegmental area. Here cells create dopamine, a natural stimulant, and share it with other regions of the brain – creating a sort of reward system. She says: 'It's below your emotions. It's... associated with wanting, with motivation, with focus on and craving. In fact, the same brain region where activity becomes active when you feel the rush of cocaine.' Add a 'comedy spin' to these analysts' observations and factoids – and the plots for thousands of romantic comedies come to mind.

Romance is great. It's the adventure of discovering or accepting that we're capable of deep emotions. That we can be swept away in an indescribable, euphoric feeling. Tolkien writes of fantasy in these terms – perhaps fantasy is connected to love, who knows. Comedy is great. It's built on the hope that humans, by taking action, can have a strong hand in really affecting and changing their own lives. And so – in romantic comedy – things 'work out' because someone commits to the adventure of doing something to enhance their own life. And that's <u>hopeful</u>.

Like many people, I want to believe in a special relationship that <u>can</u> make every day just a bit better. A communion with someone that, every once in a while, will be what Emily Esfahani Smith calls that 'micro-moment of positivity resonance'. Audiences respond to 'hope' and want to believe. So no wonder I never tire of watching the great romcoms – films such as *City Lights*, *It Happened One Night*, *The Philadelphia Story*, *Divorce – Italian Style*, *Annie Hall*, *Moonstruck*, *When Harry Met Sally*, *Four Weddings and a Funeral*, *Hors de Prix*, *Bridget Jones' Diary*, *Bride and Prejudice* and *Tanghi Argentini*.

Authors Helen Jacey and Craig Batty avidly investigate screenwriting practices. I have been privileged to hear their talks and be part of their discussions on the craft and art of screenwriting in academic and professional screenwriting settings. I've witnessed their ability to cull nuggets of insight and to break down relevant factors into understandable, <u>useful</u> tools. This book will be an <u>adventure</u> for you and as they call for new innovation in structures, tone and approaches, will give us all hope that the romantic comedy will live on and prosper.

INTRODUCTION

Have you ever had a romantic comedy dream? Not the physical steamy kind – we all have those! We're talking about the kind where your now-pain-in-the-ass significant other appears as they once were, before months turned into years and 'Your turn to load the dishwasher, babe' came to have a more resoundingly familiar ring than 'You complete me, my darling'?

Us neither – as appealing as it sounds!

Fantasy and desire are why romantic comedy is alive and kicking, and probably isn't going anywhere soon. Now more than ever, romantic comedy surrounds us. Big screens, little screens, tablets and phones... it's virtually impossible to run away from light-hearted love stories in all their evolutions and permutations, across all platforms, apps and ads. Dating websites use romantic comedy to advertise their services on underground trains, and to run viral campaigns. In feature film more specifically, the romcom is still thriving across the globe, from Hollywood to Bollywood to Nollywood.

What does this exciting proliferation of the romcom mean for you, dear reader/writer? Perhaps you're consulting this book because you intend to write a romcom feature, or are at least exploring the idea. Maybe you've chosen a character or a concept for your screenplay, and it feels like a romcom but you're not sure. Or maybe you're seeking inspiration or answers to creative or commercial dilemmas. Alternatively, maybe you work in film development and are interested in new views and new models – resources to inspire and inform the development process of projects you're working on. Or maybe you're a student looking for insights that will inspire and shape your ideas about writing in this genre, from a creative rather than a mere 'critical' perspective.

Whoever you are, we hope that this book comes as something of a refreshing surprise. The idea to write it together also came as something of a surprise to us, and has taken us on our own 'chumcom' journey. As writers ourselves, we both wanted to write a book for screenwriters about creating stories that come with certain expectations to illuminate just how broad the romantic comedy genre can be. By sharing with you approaches and principles of writing, by questioning aspects of produced romcoms, and by having some fun along the way (as we have writing it!), we hope to inspire and re-energise your own stories and ideas.

Perhaps unfairly, writing a romantic comedy can come with a little more baggage than other genres. It's the genre that can make people cringe, angry, or look at you askance if you claim to be writing one. On the other hand, lots of people will cry out that they love romcoms and can't watch anything else. Sometimes the biggest assumption even writers can make is that you'll be creating something formulaic – a boy-meets-girl scenario, or a story full of dubious gender representations. There's something about romantic comedy's unique blend of a lightness of tone and obsessively relentless emotional terrain that presses buttons or brings a smile, depending on people's attitudes. It is true, however, that some romcoms can be over-formulaic, predictable and sugary sweet, with the ubiquitous happy ending in which soulmates commit for life at a big fat rich wedding! What's key to remember as writers is that what repels some people might actually provide a really fun night out for others.

The romcom is therefore a genre that people tend to love or hate, a bit like the horror and the thriller. Audiences tend not to categorise drama, biopic and comedy in the same way. Romantic comedy can be viewed more rigidly than other genres. There's something of a lasting myth about the film version of the genre – that a 'proper' romcom must meet certain expectations such as having polarised characters and classic turning points, like cute meets, the lovers seeing the light and finding enduring happiness. For writers, romantic comedy screenplays are possibly more vulnerable to the age-old problem of genre definition – and a need to see certain boxes being ticked when it comes to story types, character arcs, endings and themes.

The kind of romcom you want to write will ultimately depend on what you like to watch yourself. Hopefully, this book will radicalise and revitalise your approach to writing screenplays in the genre by exploring how you can make your work delightful, original and uniquely your own take on love. We're committed to helping you write a romcom that inspires you, reflects what you want to say about love and the human condition, and is ultimately an enjoyable journey – for you and your eventual audience.

Our approach to writing the romcom is that the first draft is *your draft*. Other than saying, 'It's probably one day going to be defined as a romcom', our approach is to focus on the ideas around your comedic love story. We'll explore certain familiar elements of the romcom from the perspective of writing practice, but these aim to help you question your work, not limit it. Although it might seem strange, we want to quash any rules and regulations you might be carrying around about the romcom. This is because our approach with this book is one of finding your way through development by trying, experiencing, thinking and then thinking some more. We want your story to develop organically, from the point of view of your perspectives on the world, life, love and relationships, and ideas about them that you want to explore. Ideation is, we feel, a core aspect of development. So, while we'll be giving you lots of information about the craft of the romcom, we really want to help you get excited about your ideas. Audiences go to see films because they're interested in ideas – in what the world has to offer us as human beings – so you, too, need to be a master of ideas.

Audiences crave reinvention and stimulation and it's your job to tune into the zeitgeist, to mine all your creative faculties, and to put your stamp on love and romance, whatever your particular sensibility might be – crazy, quirky, cynical or upbeat. What worked five years ago might not necessarily work today. Not only do our values and attitudes change, we are living in darker, less secure and more ambivalent times. This can make us retreat to feel-good and to tradition – or it can make us more cynical. Today there is more gender equality in the Western world, and what was 'the battle of the sexes' is better termed a 'constantly renegotiated truce' between men and women. Not to mention the fact that audiences rightly expect romantic comedies to feature gay, bisexual and transgender couples. Nobody knows anything, as William Goldman, writer of arch bromance *Butch Cassidy and the Sundance Kid*, so saliently reminds us. And nobody has all the answers in terms of what will make a great contemporary romantic comedy. All we ask of you – as a screenwriter or someone working with screenwriters – is to detach yourself from any negative connotations or preconceptions you might have about the romcom.

In return, we'll bring you a fertile and eclectic mix of creative, critical and commercial perspectives to aid and inspire the development of your own project, whether it's a spec script, a commissioned project, or you're just playing around with ideas. We do make some 'assumptions' in this book, and these are:

1. Romantic comedy frequently finds a BIG audience.

2. Romantic comedy can press the buttons of some critics for being too… well, romantic.

3. Humans need nurture and intimacy and romance and sex, but not necessarily in that order, and not all the time, or in any given lifetime.

4. We all have a right to equal rights – including our characters.

5. Society and culture influence our experiences, values and attitudes about love, romance, family and commitment – and those of our characters.

6. Psychoanalytic theorists (e.g. Sigmund Freud, Jessica Benjamin, Melanie Klein) offer screenwriters some very useful models (not rules) to help us think creatively about character, sexuality and unconscious desires – and, of course, love!

7. Writers are products of their unique life experience as well as their place and time in the world, but their characters and the worlds they write are products of their imagination.

We hope you enjoy reading and working with this book, and that most of all it will add some zest to your romantic comedy screenplay.

WHY ROMANTIC COMEDY?

A glance through the history of storytelling attests to our need to reflect on the follies and foibles of the human heart from a light if not comedic point of view. There are romcom elements to be found in a Sapphic poem and an Aristophanes comedy, where women ban sex in the name of peace. Even Chaucer gets down and dirty in the dismal Middle Ages, creating a Wife of Bath whose surprisingly radical episodic spin on casual sex can still raise eyebrows. Shakespeare found his own angle on matters of the heart with a comedic take on cross-dressing and frolics in forests. Putting it bluntly, humans have sex, hormones, form close attachments and create families of all different kinds – and writers try to make sense of these, and sometimes choose comedy to do so.

The impulse to write romantic comedy stories can take the form of a wish for our own lives – an antidote for the chaos or isolation around us. Creating romantic worlds and situations can remind us we're in control – of our emotional destinies at least. Sometimes we can describe the simple goal of finding someone to travel along the bumpy road with, which might end in enduring love and commitment or simply show how passing strangers can make us feel better about ourselves and our lives. Creating a romantic comedy can also allow our imagination to play, to create, to take us out of the monotony of humdrum life, and to submerge ourselves unashamedly in feel-good and heartfelt emotions that normal life somehow represses.

In her book *Romantic Comedy*, Claire Mortimer (2010) explains how romantic comedy films show the wider changes going on in society. For instance, from the 1930s to the 1950s, finding love in order to get married was the be-all and end-all of romcoms, reaching a matrimonial pressure point with Doris Day and her pink pyjamas and pillow talk. The rise of feminism has had a huge impact on how we think about gender difference, sex and sexuality, love and marriage, with big implications for the romantic comedy. From the late 1990s onwards, the female protagonist began to dominate the genre, in stories that focused on her problems in life and in love. *Sex and the City*, *27 Dresses*, *Confessions of a Shopaholic*, *Last Holiday* and *Juno* are good examples. They could be termed romantic dramedies but often go by the broader term 'chick flick'.

But you can't keep a good man down, and the era of the bromcom soon dawned. Certainly, male heterosexual pairings have been around for many decades in film and TV shows, such as *Butch Cassidy and the Sundance Kid*, *Cheers* (Norm and Cliff's pairing) and the various renditions of Sherlock and Watson. *Sideways* launched the 'bromcom', the male equivalent of the chick flick or girl buddy movie, which has since been followed up with films such as *Pineapple Express*, *I Love You, Man* and *Due Date*.

Fast forward to today, where the romantic comedy encompasses bromcom (boy buddies), zomromcom (zombie romantic comedies) and sorocom (girl buddies). The list of ever-evolving hybrids will only get longer – and though this might all seem like a bunch of convenient buzz words for marketing campaigns, it does go some way in showing that, like thriller and horror, the romantic comedy has finally ascended to the status of a 'super-genre'.

There's a writer behind all these stories. Somebody originated the germ of an idea and brought it to life. 'Romantic comedy' thus becomes a catch-all label for the myriad stories where a writer has chosen comedy to come up with a protagonist or group of protagonists who have a major and all-consuming problem with *somebody else* (or *something else*), who appears to be the source of all problems but who really is only trouble because of unresolved issues in the protagonist. Dealing with *somebody else* and finding yourself in the process takes up most of the time and effort in the modern romcom. As Jean-Paul Sartre so eloquently said, 'Hell is other people.' If other people are the hell of romantic comedy, the best route out of purgatory is healing yourself first. In this respect, creating one might involve you finding out more about yourself and love than you expected!

Romcoms have definitely become edgier, quirkier, darker, dirtier and steamier in recent years. Films such as *Moonrise Kingdom*, *Before Midnight*, *Silver Linings Playbook* and *(500) Days of Summer* reflect writers finding unexplored terrain and asking new questions. Taboos are no longer off limits with the advent of gross-out comedy, subversive storylines and ambiguity of meaning. Boundaries keep shifting and today it's not uncommon for one film to encompass many different tones, types of comedy and more subtle and ambiguous emotional arcs where characters' love can grow over years. And despite the now very old cliché that romance is for women, a lot more male protagonists crave love and affection in this super-genre today. But do we give male romantic comedy heroes more fun and freedom than females – are 'guy' problems in love different to 'girl' ones?

SUB-GENRES, TYPES AND HYBRIDS

Art is not science, and genre theory and its focus on categorisation and labels demonstrates how the critical/rational mind likes to find a way of making sense of story types. As we want to emphasise, labelling or categorising your romcom project in generic terms too early in the development process can actually box you in, and cause too many limitations or anxieties early on. Alternatively, if you're purposely setting out to fuse two or three genres in a way that hasn't been done before, it can help to explore those other genres first. Hybrids can soar – and they can fall on their swords. *Shaun of the Dead* is a bromedy/zomromcom and was a big hit. *Silver Linings Playbook* – a dramedy/famromcom – ditto. Reviews were far more mixed about *This Means War*, an espionage/romcom, and *Killers*, an espionage/action/romcom.

Sometimes your genre can change and evolve during development, depending on where you take the protagonist and the kind of journey you give them. A two-hander might turn into a bromcom, for example, or a combination thereof. *Bridesmaids*, for example, is a dramedy/romantic comedy but not quite a romantic dramedy. It follows Annie as she comes to terms with her best friend's marriage, and has to deal with her own low self-esteem. Part of this process, but not central to it, is her relationship with a traffic cop. When Annie finally forgives herself and manages to change her negative outlook of the world, she's ready to engage in a non-self-destructive relationship with a man who cares for her instead of using her.

The Hangover is a bromcom/chumcom with a small element of romcom. It follows as its central story drive a group of guys who are old friends – some brothers – on a stag week. The small romcom element comes through Stu the dentist's storyline. He has a bully and nag of a wife and on his journey finds love with a 'tart with a heart' single mother hooker.

Imagine a film where a hen party encounters a stag party. Depending on what happens and who the protagonists are, the screenplay could be sold as a romcom, a bromcom, a chumcom, a dramedy – or a combination of them all!

Let's start by looking at some of the most popular genre labels for the films we want to write that deal with matters of the heart in a comedic way.

THE CLASSIC ROMCOM

Boy and Girl (or same-sex version) meet each other and, after largely emotional trials and tribulations, come together by the end. These stories are all about finding your soulmate and permanently healing the emotional scars that have got in the way of finding love previously. The classic romantic comedy can be high-concept, where the writer firmly places the main character in a situation riddled with conflict and dramatic irony to push them into being forced to change. *Pretty Woman*, *When Harry Met Sally* and *Sleepless in Seattle* were pre-millennial boy-meets-girl Hollywood films that set the standard for the classic romcom. We can call them classic romcoms because of their cute meets and predictable endings of the couple's union. More recent versions include *What Happens in Vegas*, *The Proposal* and *The Five-Year Engagement*.

The DNA of the classic romcom includes:

- Both characters have almost equal story space.
- Friends, family or colleagues usually act as allies and saboteurs to the brewing romance.
- Both have inner conflicts – low self-esteem, bitterness, fear of failure, etc. – preventing them from relating well to potential dates.
- These inner conflicts can be healed by the positive and opposite aspects of the other main character.
- Despite outer conflicts, they battle their way through clashes to finally learn the other one is in fact their soulmate.
- There's a very happy ending.

THE ROMANTIC DRAMEDY

Boy meets Girl has evolved into the solo protagonist (of any gender) with a problem – and this problem gets in the way of them forming a relationship with anybody, let alone the person who might be staring them in the face. Sometimes the romantic aspect to a dramedy revolves around loss or loneliness, and the challenge is for the protagonist to learn to have a better relationship with him or herself. Hope for a better relationship in the future can come as a kind of reward for the hard emotional work the protagonist has undertaken through the story.

Protagonists can be male or female in the romantic dramedy, but the female protagonist in particular has come into her own with a big focus on internal conflicts that create outer issues. Woody Allen's relationship comedies fall into this category, where his main characters go on journeys of self-exploration triggered by the irritants or worse of other people. The 'significant other' in a dramedy – the one who causes problems – can be another woman. Examples include *In Her Shoes*, where a sister is the cause of resentment, and *Bridesmaids*, where the loss of a friend who's getting married is the trigger to a downward spiral for the protagonist. In *Last Holiday*, store assistant Georgia finds out she's going to die, and decides to liquidate her life savings to treat herself to the luxury holiday she's never been able to take. Her reward is learning how deeply loved she is – and that she isn't going to die after all!

The DNA of the romantic dramedy includes:

- There's a dominant protagonist whom the audience is encouraged to relate to through use of POV.
- Internal conflicts, often relating to self-esteem, get in the way of self-respect and ability to love.
- External conflicts come in the form of job, family, friends, children or an out of the ordinary gift.
- The story doesn't necessarily end with union, but often does.

THE BROMCOM

Formerly known as the male buddy movie, the bromcom gives male audiences a window on male friendship, emulating the familiar patterns of romcoms or romantic dramedies. In these stories, Boy meets potential male friend but internal conflicts get in the way of a good friendship. Often the male protagonist has low-self-esteem issues, something triggered by his inner (often unconscious) conflicts around conventional masculinity. He could be a 'loser', as far from the alpha male romantic hero as you can get.

Bromcoms can involve a romantic element in the form of a relationship with a woman, and the journey of friendship has a knock-on positive effect on the male protagonist's capacity to be a better boyfriend. Bromcoms can also be ensemble stories, where a group of guys go through a bonding experience and emerge with a better sense of who they are. Examples include *The Hangover* and *21 & Over*.

The DNA of the bromcom includes:

- The protagonist (or protagonists) is male and straight.
- The protagonist's opposite number is a male, with very different traits at first glance.
- The males become very good, if not best, friends.
- Relationships with females are secondary to the main story.

THE SOROCOM

Perhaps it is time for the sorocom to come into its own, away from its overgeneralised 'chick flick' label or the non-female-specific 'dramedy' category. *In Her Shoes*, *Frances Ha* and any film that tells a story and celebrates the need for women and friendship, particularly the uniqueness of female friendship, without a complicated romance as subplot, would be the defining DNA. In other words, a genuinely female equivalent of the bromcom. *The Heat* is an example of an action sorocom, where two tough female cops form an unlikely partnership – and there are going to be quite a few more of those as women leads continue to enter action and crime territory in roles that aren't just victim, love interest, or nasty antagonist.

THE CHUMCOM

Similar to the bromcom but without the straight male emphasis, the chumcom could be a term for those films that focus on platonic, odd-couple partnerships that involve either the same sex or the opposite sex. 'Chum' is the word – there's no romantic or sexual subtext, or, if there is, it tends not to take over. That said, Julio and Tenoch in *Y Tu Mamá También* did end up in a passionate embrace, which on one hand was the logical conclusion of a raw and competitive friendship, but on the other hand put a stop to their friendship.

Chumcoms essentially poke fun at the headaches that working partnerships or friendships can cause. Again, the trials and tribulations of the friendship are under scrutiny here and function as the main cause of outer problems. *Identity Thief*, *My Best Friend's Wedding* and *Gayby* are examples of chumcoms.

The DNA of the chumcom includes:

- A pair of protagonists with opposite traits, or a group of friends with diverse traits, are pushed together.
- In spite of inner or outer conflicts, the protagonists end up best of friends – or at the very least they learn to respect each other.
- The story doesn't lead to sexual love and the protagonists can go their separate ways.

THE FAMCOM

A comedic focus on the problems caused by families is an offshoot of dramedy. The protagonist has to deal with issues that being with their families creates or triggers, or long unresolved family wounds finally come to an ugly and often hilarious head. The family is the main source of conflict in this type of story, where 'You can't live with them and you can't live without them' is the modus operandi. The family can also be that of the protagonist's loved one – where potential or actual in-laws reveal the nightmare that they inevitably will be, such as in *The Family Stone*. *Guilt Trip* is another example of the famcom, where a son goes on a road trip with his mother that ultimately leads to them breaking entrenched dynamics, and understanding and appreciating one another a lot more than before the journey. The journey results in healthier self-esteem for both mother and son, and a better way of connecting with other people. This is also the case in *The Descendants*, in which a father develops a better relationship with his daughters.

Where it's the family causing relationship problems between the protagonist and their partner, the 'famcom' might be more accurately termed a 'famromcom'. A successful forerunner of this type was *Meet the Parents*. The films *2 Days in Paris* and *2 Days in New York* might also be considered famromcoms in that the female protagonist and her partner are put under huge pressure by the demanding and conflictual dynamics generated by her demanding and ever-present French family.

The DNA of the famcom includes:

- A protagonist who needs to get a life and/or a relationship, but who has a nightmare family (or extended family) who cannot be got rid of (usually whose members also need a life or need to change).
- Separation from, and reacceptance of, the family unit.
- If there's a romantic angle, the partnership finally comes before the family members, who accept they no longer come first.

THE BIOROMCOM

The possibilities for genre hybrids are endless. Take for example *Julie & Julia* – a delightful biopic/comedy/chumcom/romcom. The romcom element comes from the enduring and comedic love story between Julia and her husband. The chumcom comes from Julie having Julia as her muse.

The DNA of a bioromcom includes:

- The plot revolves around a famous, or relatively well-known, true-life character.
- Internal and external conflicts affect the character's ability to find or maintain loving relationships.
- A secondary main character is a significant other to the main character (wife, secret affair, soulmate).

- The love affair is affected, even threatened, by the main character's occupation/area of achievement in the outside world.

Without running the risk of getting into silly territory, we might even suggest that there are more types of romcom on our screens today, with more types to come. These can and might include:

- **Zomromcom** – a humorous romantic dramedy about love with a zombie, as seen in *Warm Bodies*

- **Periodromcom** – all the more original for taking what could be a biopic drama and replacing it with a romantic comedy, such as *Shakespeare in Love*

- **Gerontocom** – stories that dwell on the emotional lives and romances of older people, as seen in *Something's Gotta Give* and *Hope Springs*

- **Musical romcom** – films such as *Moulin Rouge* and those from Bollywood

- **Oddcom** – the love of a non-human object, such as *Ted*, *Her* and *Ruby Sparks*

As we can see, sometimes it can just be a case of adding a romantic storyline to another genre in order to shake it up and give the screenplay saleability. For example, the romance in *RED* gave what might have been a geronto action movie a gerontocom flavour.

What next, we might ask? Scificom? Paranormacom? Perhaps these already exist – and maybe you're already writing one yourself...

QUICK **INSIGHT**

Andrew Horton is the Jeanne H Smith Professor of Film and Media Studies at the University of Oklahoma, an award-winning screenwriter, and the author of 30 books on film, screenwriting and cultural studies.

Some of my favourite romantic comedies

Never on Sunday. I knew Melina Mercouri and Jules Dassin personally, but it's not because of just that. Jules was blacklisted and went to live in France. He wrote, directed and starred in *Never on Sunday* with his wife, Milena, about an American coming to Greece. He's called Homer, in love with ancient Greece, and then he falls in love with a prostitute. He tries to change her so he can 'be' ancient Greece, but she's dealing with modern Greece. He was blacklisted – you don't get the romantic comedy ending at the end. She finally tells him, just when you're waiting for the happy ending, 'Homer, go home.' Fantastic!

One of my favourite people is Preston Sturges, so *The Lady Eve* is way up there for me. I love that romantic comedy formula that the women are usually cleverer than the guys. She's just trying to screw the money out of him, and yes, of course, they do fall in love. Very different people, they somehow work it out, but it plays with the genre at the end.

Last one, but not least – *The Day I Became a Woman*, an Iranian film, with three stories with three females. One is a little girl who can't play anymore because she's about to become ten. She asks her grandmother, 'What time is it?' and she works out she's got one hour to be a girl and play with her male friends. At the end of the film, her mother dresses her in adult Muslim women's clothes.

The end of *Fargo* tells you it's a romantic comedy, too. 'I love you.' 'I love you too.' It's all in the ending.

EXERCISE – KNOW YOUR GENRE

Use the following premise and flesh it out in different ways to change its genre potential, from a) a classic romcom, to b) a bromcom or a sorocom, and then to c) a famcom. You'll need to look at each genre and change things like protagonist, world, journey and theme accordingly.

Tom is a workaholic. Since leaving university, he's climbed the management ladder and moved from company to company to give himself new challenges and earn more money. Larissa is also a high-achiever but, unlike Tom, doesn't work hard at all – she's a genius who can turn water into wine. She's thought about having a family but isn't sure what she wants her role in life to be. Tom and Larissa meet one lunchtime at a trendy sandwich shop – where both of them want the last dark rye sourdough roll.

MATTERS OF THE HEART

From the quantity and quality of romcoms in the marketplace, the appeal of stories about the simple challenge of connecting intimately with another, and the need for true friendships, it's obvious that the genre isn't going away any time soon. Romcoms offer a wide variety of films that meet deep human needs, and the proliferation of romcom types means that you, the writer, can choose and develop a story that reflects what you want to say about the human need for connection – albeit in a light tone – without too many restrictions. *The Other Woman*, *My Best Friend's Wedding*, *(500) Days of Summer*, *Monster-in-Law* and *Before Midnight* all tell very different stories and to some extent appeal to very different audiences.

Serving matters of the heart, the romcom is a genre that's all about negotiating what it means to be human and connect with others. It's complicated enough being human today and managing your own life, let alone sharing it with other people. But as we've discussed, the blurred lines between romantic comedy, romantic dramedy (or dramantic comedy) and dramedy suggest that we need stories, now more than ever, about our lonely and confused identities and the problems they can create in connecting with others.

Romcoms can tell these stories and satisfy audiences through original characters, compellingly emotional stories, diverse comedic tones, familiar and unfamiliar worlds and a host of distinctive styles.

WORLD CINEMA

Is romantic comedy a Hollywood-dominated genre? Undoubtedly, most of the hallmark classic romcoms have emerged out of the US over decades, from the studio-produced screwballs of the 1930s, right up to today's indies, such as *Ruby Sparks* and *(500) Days of Summer.* But just as love is a human condition that knows no boundaries, romantic comedies, where love is explored with humour, emerge out of almost every filmmaking culture. In the UK, the film production company Working Title has achieved huge success with a string of Richard Curtis romantic comedies, including *Four Weddings and a Funeral*, *Love Actually*, *Notting Hill* and *About Time*, not to mention the *Bridget Jones* franchise. In France, romantic comedies abound. International hits include *Amelie*, *I Do*, *Populaire*, *Romantics Anonymous*, *2 Days in Paris* and *The Draw*. And no, they aren't all set in Paris, the city of romance! From further afield, Nollywood – the Nigerian film industry – has a long tradition of the romantic comedy. *Flower Girl* is a classic but recent romcom set in Lagos, in which Kemi pursues marriage with career-obsessed Umar and gets the help of superstar Tunde to help her in her mission.

But it's Bollywood that's dominated the output of what we might call the musical romantic dramedy. Indian culture seems to thrive on stories of the heart, where love and family take precedence over work and careers. This has resulted in a vast number of 'epic' musical romantic dramedies, many of them lasting for three or four hours and, unfortunately, not a lot of them 'making it' in Western culture. But things are changing, and many of today's Bollywood films are embracing – for better or for worse – more 'Western' tropes of storytelling. And here's where the romantic comedy really has potential.

The recent film *2 States* is a good example of this pretty major shift. It's well structured and well paced – and it's really funny! The story follows Krish, a Punjabi MBA student, who meets Ananya, a student from South India. And here's where the comedy begins. In true romcom fashion, Krish and Ananya fall in love – but what's interesting about this story, set in the context of Indian culture, is that the comedy and conflict come mainly from their parents' reactions to the relationship, not just the situations they find themselves in. It's a story of North versus South, with Krish and Ananya representing both the traditions of and the prejudices towards their respective states. And so, after some initial comedic conflict relating to their own perspectives on the relationship, it's a case of 'bring in the parents and let the comedy ensue!' It's expected in Indian culture that sons and daughters have the utmost respect for elders – and so Krish and Ananya's love is tested by their loyalty to their parents and their culture. Beliefs, values, habits and expectations thus provide ample fuel for comedic conflict. Whether it's related to eating habits, dress tastes or educational abilities, this film puts its protagonists on a hilarious journey to find acceptance, happiness and love.

With a slightly more 'out there' story, *Queen* follows the story of Rani, a 24-year-old living in Delhi, who, two days before her wedding, is jilted by her fiancé, Vijay. In the context of Indian culture, this kind of 'shunning' is a pretty big issue. And so for Rani, who comes from a conservative and proud family – who are just learning about webcams! – her world really has come crashing down. She nevertheless bites the bullet and decides to go on the honeymoon to Europe that she and Vijay had already booked. This begins for her a journey of discovery, where, although there are hints of romance with new friend Oleksander, the person she really falls in love with is herself. Rani meets many friends on her adventure, leading to comedic encounters in nightclubs, tourist spots and at food stalls.

But through these raucous scenes, Rani learns about freedom and self-belief. This is emphasised by mentor character, Vijayalakshmi, a French-Spanish--Indian woman who works in the hotel where Rani is staying. Seeing the very different lifestyle she leads – including sex, smoking, drinking and dancing – Rani learns about life, and how to respect herself. Her emotional arc is that she'll no longer be at the beck-and-call of a man like Vijay – which, of course, also says something about traditional Indian culture.

Queen might therefore be best described as a romantic dramedy, and follows other films such as *Waitress, Goddess* and *Leap Year* – films in which, amongst the comedy and the romance or flirtation, the real story (theme) is about learning to love oneself as a prerequisite to a good relationship.

QUICK **INSIGHT**

Stayci Taylor, a screenwriter, playwright and comedian researching female perspectives in mainstream comedy screenplays for her PhD at RMIT University.

What does romance look like in the 21st century?

There's still an expectation that women in romantic comedies should not only be partial to the idea of marriage, but desperate for it, leaving male characters with a plethora of infinitely more interesting options. Most of these involve escaping the marriage trap – whether to maintain their slacker lifestyle (spend more time with the boys) – or maintain their playboy lifestyle (spend more time with the girls). That these narratives trade exclusively upon what women are supposed to *be like* and what men are supposed to *be like* reflects little of the 21st century world we live in, and are reductive for both our female and male characters – although at least the men aren't restricted by a very narrow set of age, size and beauty criteria.

Most romantic comedies still cling to the wedding as an inevitable resolution, which fails to reflect the more complex and fascinating desires in a diverse 21st century reality. And, worse, this contributes to a popular cultural landscape already saturated in narratives where only heterosexual, monogamous, procreative relationships will result in any sort of contentment – especially for women – thus creating subtle or not-so-subtle unease in those who live outside those frameworks by either choice or circumstance.

Add to this the ubiquity of middle-class, white characters in well-heeled suburbs and it's no wonder we find ourselves unable to differentiate between one romantic comedy and another – they all blur into one mass of bridal fittings and contrived, gender-based misunderstandings. That's not to say there can't be well-crafted, funny and pleasurable romantic comedies with all of the above elements. But they work best, I think, when the writer is committed to a certain cultural specificity – I rarely tire of watching Nora Ephron's New York or Richard Curtis's London. But how invigorated might the genre be if infused with every writer's unique perspectives?

When Nia Vardalos remained true to hers for *My Big Fat Greek Wedding*, the box office spoke for itself. And, amongst some of the many fine features of that screenplay – including a female protagonist who shared the ordinary, struggling character traits that serve comedy so well (usually reserved for male characters) – the wedding of the title wasn't an unquestioned inevitability, but a dilemma, given voice to in a narrative so culturally specific that the pressure on the character to get married wasn't assumed to be universal.

What *is* universal, of course, is love – and it's a missed opportunity for the romantic comedy genre that so few reveal the multiple ways in which love manifests in people's lives, beyond straight, white, marriage-focused, gender-stereotypical narratives. Of course, writing the script is no guarantee of getting the film made, but I still believe the romantic comedy screenplay that idiosyncratically embraces one of the many and varied ways people find love – within their own circles, circumstances, cities, communities, campuses, cultures, countries and, increasingly, computers – might liberate a slew of even more refreshing romantic comedy narratives beyond desperate white women chasing reluctant white men.

CASE STUDY: *THE SESSIONS*

The Sessions is a heartfelt romantic dramedy about Mark, a writer who was left severely disabled after contracting childhood polio and who lives most of his life in an iron lung, supported by carers. It's essentially about a man who wants to lose his virginity, but who can't move his body, let alone touch himself. A very human-centred dramatic irony shapes the situation of this rare protagonist. Mark's physical longings form what Giglio calls the 'inappropriate goal' of comedy. He wants to have sex, so determines he needs to pay for it, when what he really needs is to feel somebody can fall in love with him for who he is inside.

The tone of *The Sessions* is, overall, dramedic with some hilarious moments. The film features a unique blend of dark humour, wit, withering remarks, irony, sarcasm, irreverence, self-deprecation and cringe-making physical humour, which lifts it from the dramatic pathos of Mark's acute sense of loneliness and powerlessness. The emotional tone could be called 'compassionate' with some 'awkwardness' thrown into the mix, which is mainly achieved through the complex characterisation of Mark and the people who care for him and on whom he practically and emotionally depends. We're able to get to know him from many different angles, but most importantly from his own perspective via the use of voice-over.

Mark is first introduced to us in old footage of his graduation, where he crosses the stage on a gurney. We're told by the anchorman how Mark's determination teaches us that 'courage and perseverance overcome obstacles'. Mark's voice-over quickly takes charge – he introduces himself to us along with his very specific world view. His night-time companions are his iron lung, his computer and the cat that comes in to sit on his breathing machine in lieu of a lap. When the cat's fur tickles him, we're let into the infinite challenges of Mark's unique reality – 'Shit. Scratch with your mind. Scratch with your mind.'

This, just like the anchorman's words, is loaded with double meaning in a story about one man's quest to achieve physical intimacy. At this early point, Mark believes he's doomed to only scratch any itch with his mind. *The Sessions* is all about Mark's journey to becoming a vibrant sexual man, who learns to love his body and to be able to give pleasure to women. He calls his carer a 'crazy bitch' who he wants to sack because she makes him feel powerless. In revenge, he gets an erection when she's washing him and fantasises about getting rid of her. Mark turns to new priest Father Brendan for spiritual guidance on the matter, worried about his own petty need for vengeance, telling him 'I believe in God with a sense of humour' in reference to his own state. Father Brendan, a practical man, advises Mark to go ahead with the dismissal and 'find someone nice'.

Mark's relationship with his priest is based on spiritual guidance, friendship and, on Father Brendan's side, non-judgemental empathy and moral dilemma. It's to him that Mark discloses he has a shelf life, and that he's a virgin. He doesn't want to die without being close to a woman, yet can't do anything about his private desires in a conventional sense – or so he believes. With all situations in his life other than the freedom of his mind, he depends on others to carry out his will. Mark convinces himself that this obviously very human 'goal' is all he needs, and, in a way, we the audience are convinced by it too. But this is really a smokescreen for a deeper need for human connection. When he falls in love with the replacement carer, Amanda, and declares his love for her, she can't cope with his request to take their relationship further – not least because she has a boyfriend. Amanda is replaced by Chinese, stoic and seemingly humourless Vera, who's not the conventional pretty girl he dreams of touching and kissing.

Mark's solution seems to be paying for sex with a surrogate – someone skilled in working with physically challenged people. Cheryl, the surrogate, is a caring, professional and sensitive woman. She's also married to her philosopher househusband and they have one son. It's through Cheryl's point of view, combined with Mark's voice-over, that we follow their journey through the planned six therapy sessions. Cheryl is determined to keep up professional boundaries, while Mark's feelings become more complex. His goal of sex is sharply contrasted with his obvious need for emotional intimacy and a real relationship. We also understand that his loneliness is due not just to his incarceration in the iron lung and his disabled state, but also to his immense guilt that his sister died in childhood.

Cheryl is the only person to connect with Mark as a human being first and foremost, who sees the man, the little hurt boy inside who needs to forgive himself, and the lover who desperately needs reciprocated love. Despite her best efforts to keep things professional, Cheryl's compassion is soon aroused by Mark. He actively, and somewhat charismatically, transgresses the boundaries and wants a date, before declaring his love in the form of a 'love poem to nobody in particular'. Cheryl's husband discovers the letter and they fight, only for Cheryl to realise that she's crossed the emotional line with Mark. The break-up is inevitable, both of them equally conflicted. They terminate the six sessions at the fifth, and Mark descends into heartbreak and loneliness. One night, when his generator breaks down, Mark loses oxygen and nearly dies. It's at the hospital that he meets volunteer Susan and relates to her as an attractive woman. Here we see the extent to which Cheryl has facilitated Mark's new sexual confidence and determination to connect with women as a man who feels equal, rather than the self-hating fantasist of his former self. We later find out that Mark marries Susan, who becomes the love of his life until his death several years later.

The Sessions is about a man in an awful, lifelong situation with seemingly no way out. He depends on the goodwill of strangers until a non-judgemental, unique human being arrives in his life and helps him heal his physical and emotional wounds. Just like the priest, Cheryl shows another side to Mark – the vulnerability and fear behind the witty, defensive and self-deprecating tone. Everyone who cares for Mark is given point of view, so their understandings, dilemmas and concerns are shared with us. This multidimensional perspective achieves a depth of humanity that is profound and shows how diverse and deep a 'romantic comedy' can go.

The sheer warmth of the tone of *The Sessions* is also achieved by a focus on the connection between people, where conflicts are gentle but internal conflicts are potentially 'life' threatening. Death looms, but it's never described with fear, dread or self-pity – only pathos, wit and acceptance. Susan, Vera, Cheryl and Amanda, each in their own way, are caring, coping, nurturing, feeling, connecting, respecting, reflecting, and sharing Mark's ordeal with him. There are very few scenes where the 'ego' creates conflict and, where these do exist, they usually involve tertiary characters. The dominant actions taken by all the characters are fundamentally compassionate and non-aggressive.

After Mark dies, even the cat, his nightly visitor, sits on his empty iron lung, missing his presence. Like the cat, we miss Mark and value his contribution to our lives because this compassionate romantic dramedy has let us in, to share his journey intimately – without overt manipulation, but with plenty of honest emotional truth, tender respect for individuals and clever wit.

HOT TIPS

- Watch examples – current and past – of the different genres and sub-genres that your screenplay includes.

- Embrace the emotional world of the romcom by having a romcom weekend. Watch romcoms back-to-back, from studio films, to indies, via world cinema. Try to work out what they tell us about the period they were made in, or the culture in which they're set.

- Define the DNA of your screenplay by working out the main elements. What kinds of protagonist? What functions do secondary characters have? Where's the conflict coming from? How is it resolved?

- Why are you interested in the romcom? How does the genre help to tell your story? What are your thematic ideas and how do they relate to the romcom?

WHO'S LOOKING AT YOU, KID?

OK, so it might be a line pinched from classic romance *Casablanca*, but it's a very good question to ask of your romantic comedy project. Who will be looking at what you're creating, and why? Who will be the first to engage with your story as screenplay readers, and then hopefully as viewers of a produced film? Who are you writing for, and why? What do you hope people will gain from spending 90 minutes or more in the romcom world you've created? What are your authorial intentions?

Audiences want to watch romcoms and writers want to write them, but typically the link between audience and screenwriter are tenuous and indirect. There are many layers, people and processes between you, the writer, working on your own, and the film actually being played on a screen. Assuming you complete a good draft that you want to share with others, it can be helpful to think about different reader responses from these broad areas:

- **The Creative Challenge** – the impulse you first had in wanting to write a romcom. The energy and creative stimulation that future collaborators will share on the journey of development.

- **The Pleasure Principle** – the enjoyment levels that readers and other creators will get from being in the romantic and comedic world you've created.

- **Entertainment Factor** – the 'event' aspects of your romcom. Does it fill a role in the world of entertainment? Will your romcom be worth the effort of giving up precious time to create it, or to watch it?

- **The Business Potential** – does your romcom work as a product that can reach a big audience? What's its Unique Selling Point? Does it have franchise and/or merchandise potential?

The bottom line is that you need to know your audiences – all the groups and individuals you're ultimately writing for – and who might gain pleasure and entertainment (if not a new perspective on the meaning of life!) from your work.

Therefore, as the writer of a romcom it might be helpful to think in terms of all the stakeholders in the industry of this particular genre, and what they'll be hoping to get out of your story. How is it a creative challenge? How does your work give pleasure? How will it entertain? Who will it entertain? Does it stand a realistic chance of being made and finding an audience? Let's look in more detail at some of these audiences.

Remember, some people – including you – might be some or all of these things, as we all have to increasingly wear different hats in our 'multi-hyphenate' lives.

YOU, THE SCREENWRITER

You might never have written a romcom, or it could be your favourite genre. Whatever your motive, believe it or not, romantic comedies are as challenging to write as epic historical dramas. For example, how do you make it original and commercial, therefore appealing to investors? Writing a romcom should be fun – but it could also be painful. One thing is for sure – it'll involve immersion in highly emotional waters. There's no place for being aloof or dispassionate – writing romcom is actually for the brave-hearted.

Remember, your first audience is yourself. If you love your screenplay, the chances are good that it might go somewhere.

If it has high self-esteem, it's more likely that you'll pitch it with passion. There might then be a greater chance of it finding others who also love it. If you don't particularly like predictability and unambiguous happy endings, then why bother writing a mainstream classic romcom? It'll probably feel like your heart isn't in it. But if you love this type of story, you'll probably also love writing one, and will hopefully do a good job by drawing on both your in-depth knowledge and your creative passion.

THE SCRIPT READER

Their role is often to assess the script for other people, such as a producer or a financier. Usually they act as the first gatekeeper, so it's vital that your romcom passes their initial test. Think of script readers like dating agency personnel – they screen future clients, take the trouble to find all their good points, take into account their more negative traits, and try to be open-minded about future potential. If your screenplay is charming, attractive, functional, and knows what it is, chances are that the script reader will think someone out there is going to love the work. Easy match!

THE PRODUCER

Taking our dating agency analogy further, you and your project need to be more than a hot date – you need to be marriage material! A producer wants to have respect for and be proud of your romcom – after all, they've decided to commit to it for the long haul. A producer will need to work with you throughout development, and to package the project up to take out to directors, financiers, sales agents and distributors. They should have confidence in describing the project's originality, reach and target audience. Opening weekend box-office receipts or downloads aren't usually central to the screenwriter's decision-making processes on their first draft, but to a producer they're a vitally important part of their thinking.

THE DIRECTOR

Your film needs to appeal to the visionary talent of a director. Ideally it'll entice them through your characters, settings, and themes of the character's journey – and be an appealing and original project for their interpretation. A writer-director might have a certain 'oeuvre', such as Woody Allen or Nancy Meyers. Alternatively, a director might want to work on something completely new in terms of genre. Like you, the director is motivated by voice, creativity and bringing powerful and entertaining stories to the screen for a large audience.

SALES AGENTS AND DISTRIBUTORS

Their unique role in ensuring that as big an audience as possible goes to see your film means they have to be able to categorise and market it effectively. If there's enough interest in and commitment to the project, they may well be brought on during the development process, before any production takes place. Decisions on cast can be informed by existing box-office data. Sales agents and distributors will make use of advanced market research methods and data, and also branding and franchise approaches.

THE 'PAYING' AUDIENCE

Just as you go to see a film or choose a TV show to watch, the audience too will have expectations about your film from its advertising and marketing, all of which communicate its genre, cast, and 'vision'. If they're in the right mood, they might well choose to watch a romcom. Common reasons for this include relaxing on a Friday night, getting a group of friends together to have fun over alcohol and snacks, first dates and occasions such as Valentine's Day and Christmas. As well as this, audiences might have preferences and tastes for particular actors, story worlds and situations, and be fans of a filmmaker.

If you're stressed, threatened or lonely, do you want to see a film that reminds you of the state you're in? Or do you want to see one that helps you escape reality? Perhaps you want a bit of both – seeing ourselves through characters can be the comic relief we need. Let's face it, terrorism and the threat of alien systems are pretty scary. So is the thought of losing your house when the bank collapses; you or a loved one getting seriously ill; or any other serious and testing life event. And if these aren't enough to be fretting about, most people have pretty monotonous jobs where trying to scrape together enough disposable cash on payday is like getting blood out of a stone.

Then there's the pace of digital change – either we're born into it or are adapting to it, but the speed and nature of how we connect and communicate can take its toll. Perhaps faster and more virtual communication comes with a price tag of loneliness – as romcoms have been known to explore, from *You've Got Mail* to *Her*. Social networking can dominate our lives and even Internet dating is a virtual guessing game until you risk all and go out in real life.

THE FILM CRITIC

They'll take a subjective and critical view of your romcom, including how it embraces the genre (or not). The critic aims to inform and entertain at the same time, and will bring their own taste, opinion and bias to the party. You only have to have a quick scan through critics' reviews on a website such as www.rottentomatoes.com to see the mixed, if not downright negative, reception of many romcoms – even if they're box-office hits. It's a fair generalisation to say that most film critics don't share the perspective of the mass audience. And it's certainly not rare for some of the more 'highbrow' critics to sniff dismissively at an audience's enjoyment of such a mainstream genre. So what are the (unlikely) odds your romcom will please the critics? Will yours be the date that melts the pickiest of suitors?

THE ACADEMIC

Critics and academics have an affinity, but the academic will try to locate the screenplay or produced film 'critically'. They'll examine romcoms in relation to things such as tropes, political debates, critical contexts and theoretical frameworks. They'll find 'evidence' of ideological positioning in your text – for example, its generic codes, tropes and their implications. Most genre film theory is written from perspectives such as these – and nearly always looking at the produced film, rather than the process of creation and ideation. Romcoms frequently fall down – as we have seen – in some academics' and film critics' eyes for peddling 'unhelpful' attitudes to sex, gender and romance, for over-identifying women with the need for love and marriage, and for not doing enough to challenge convention. Like the film critic, the academic is mainly interested in audience reaction from a critical rather than a subjective point of view.

While there can certainly be value in having academic insights into your work – as in, what is your work 'doing' and 'saying'? – unless you're a creative academic or critical practitioner, you're probably not likely to step into this world. From your point of view as the one actually developing and writing the screenplay, academic writing can also inform the creative process because it allows you to see 'in action' how your work might be interpreted intellectually.

If you want to dip your toe in academic writing on the romcom, then the reading list at the end of the book will point you in the right direction. There are some good screenwriting books now available that intellectualise practice, and that are very aware of 'the industry'. These books, which we'll also list at the end of the book, try not to be redundant to writers because they focus on 'real-world' issues – craft, creativity, industry, etc. And they're aware that most screenplays are paid for and written with specific directives in mind. Overall, it's perhaps a good idea to see academics as the overly analytical or high-functioning Asperger's friend giving unemotional Spock-like rational analysis after a bad date, or a clinically minded doctor giving your sexual health the once over!

But now it's back to you – the screenwriter. Imagine how wearing all of these different hats can aid your development process. Your romcom has to be ready for the dating game with any audience. Ideally it won't have unfinished baggage, too many negative traits or personality defects – but remember as well that there's no accounting for taste!

....

EXERCISE – THE PLEASURE PRINCIPLE

Firstly, choose one of your favourite romcoms and pretend you're its screenwriter. Ask yourself:

1. How will my romcom appeal to an audience? (Character, subject matter, tone?)
2. What emotional responses do I want my audience to feel?
3. What will my audience expect? What do I want to be familiar?
4. What will my audience be surprised by? Where do I want to subvert or surprise?
5. What's entertaining about it?

Secondly, do some research about the making of the film. Read interviews and look at the special features on the DVD. Go to www.rottentomatoes.com and read critics' reviews. Go to www.boxofficemojo.com and see how the film performed. Try to find some more academic articles or books about the film, the screenwriter, the director or the genre.

When you've done this, see if your personal responses resonate with any of these findings. If they do, what does it tell you? If they don't, what does that tell you?

....

....

EXERCISE – GETTING TO KNOW YOUR PAYING AUDIENCE

In this exercise, we want you to imagine the 'groups' or 'types' of people you're going to write your film for. Try to think about the people who'll want to actively choose your romcom (as you envisage it'll be produced) to watch and enjoy.

Ask yourself the following:

1. Who's your target audience? What are these people like? Think like a marketing specialist to nail the core demographic for your film. Are they male or female? How old are they? What social and economic group do they belong to? What else would these people spend their money on?

2. Are there other audiences who might select your film for entertainment?

3. Describe all these groups in terms of their needs, from your point of view. 'Needs' can include forms of leisure, status symbols, lifestyle, types of relationship, ethics, politics and values.

4. Which aspects of your film channel these 'needs'? Is there an obvious compatibility, or a mismatch? Will your screenplay, if produced, reinforce the attitudes and values of your target audience(s)?

5. Find some examples of produced films that have been proven to satisfy this audience. Is your screenplay idea working in the same territory?

Again, there's no right and wrong to this but it's important to know. Along the selling and pitching process you will be asked 'who's the audience?' by many people.

....

QUICK **INSIGHT**

Interview with Julian Farino, director of The Oranges

What kinds of 'comedies with a romance' do you like?

The Apartment is a fantastic example for me, but it would be very hard to get a film like that made today. People don't really do dark in this genre anymore. I find the genre a great genre of cinema but it can be frustrating that some of them are so unreal. She always runs a pet shop or him a vinyl store; everything can be in that very safe world. But there's an audience for them and maybe my expectations might not be the same as the general public.

Going back, all those Cary Grant/Rosalind Russell firecracker movies were for me the great romantic comedies. Two characters who are always in opposition, spitting out dialogue at a rate of knots, fighting with each other – but the chemistry stands out. You are gunning for the two of them because they are very enjoyable together. The heart of all the good versions of this genre is that the audience should be willing them to be together.

It's not, in my opinion, a genre for films of high quality in the modern age, as so many are manipulative and superficial. Characters are too often just types with no real substance who inhabit very safe worlds and seem to be framed with bright coloured walls and twinkly lights behind them.

Why is it such a popular genre?

Who doesn't love a romance? Clearly there's an audience for them – female-led, and date-friendly. From the studios' point of view, in America they can market them because they have stars, and if the film has Jennifer Aniston or Cameron Diaz they know they're going to be able to at least have an opening weekend with a marketing campaign that puts them upfront. They wouldn't be making them if people didn't go and see them. Whether a film has legs or not depends on how good it is. I can't think of many romantic comedies that have been abiding. In the UK, for example, we still refer to *Four Weddings*, which was made 20 years ago. I would say there are some good independent romantic comedies, like *Eternal Sunshine*, or more recently I liked the Zoe Kazan film *Ruby Sparks* for its ambition, but none of the studio ones come to mind. If you see a title like *50 First Dates* or *27 Dresses*, you pretty much know what you are in for, and it won't be Manhattan...

Do you think boy meets girl is becoming extinct?

No, I don't actually, because I think it is the essence of cinema. I think the idea of two people connecting with looks and glances – that for me is the very best of cinema. It's been the staple of studio product forever. As a genre I think it probably works because in love stories the best thing is the coming together. The hard part is to sustain it. The thrill of wanting it to happen is the great thing for the audience, and films can tail off when they are together. For a romantic comedy to work, the challenge is to keep them apart, because the audience knows they are going to be together at the end. It's the thrill of the chase and the quality of the obstacles. I think the *Bridesmaids* movies are a different form; for one thing, there's a kind of vulgarity creeping in. It's not for me – it's too base – but people love it, don't they? What made *Bridesmaids* for me was Kristin Wiig's performance in-between the jokes. She was a good vulnerable heroine and you felt something for her; you had a longing for things to get better for her.

What do you think about bromancies and bromedies (e.g. *Entourage*)?

I never thought about *Entourage* in that way. I just thought the aim was to create a chemistry that allowed you to believe these four had been friends since they were ten years old. We forced them all to play off each other in the same frame so it was all one continuous take. The chemistry was foregrounded, that they knew each other so well. It's fun to be with friends that you've got history with. The idea was that they are an organism, and the scripts are so well written that we had very little to cut. What makes it boysy is they have a good life chasing hot girls in LA – that's the aspirational, wish-fulfilment side. Chemistry is key. I did a romantic comedy TV show called *Bob and Rose*, in which a gay man falls in love with a straight woman, which is a good concept for a romantic comedy, and people have talked about making it in Hollywood. Three and a half months before we shot we told the actors to spend time together, to create an energy, and when we shot I always reminded them that their choices should always be based on the fact they actually loved each other, even when they weren't in the scenes together. That for me is the key to any romantic comedy – creating a feeling for the audience that these two are right together.

Tell us what drew you to the *The Oranges*.

I liked how it defied expectations when I read the script. Here's this older man (Hugh Laurie) you could potentially say is in a mid-life crisis, hooking up with a young, beautiful woman, and yet it wasn't about him managing his male ego, it was for me about achieving honesty with the state of happiness in his life, something that many of us fail to do. I liked the idea of somehow making his journey, this pursuit of truth, noble instead of grubby. I liked the way in the script that they declare the affair, where you might have expected it to be about keeping it clandestine. For me it was about an honest pursuit of something. The film isn't a love story in a conventional sense at all; most love stories end up with the couple together whereas this film is about the legitimacy of breaking up. It's about families breaking up, the protagonists breaking up. It's a romance that takes place in a particular bubble that in other circumstances wouldn't have got them together. She's got her tail between her legs and is feeling vulnerable, and she catches him in a moment of unhappiness in his own life which causes them to be together at this particular moment. I had fought to have Hugh in the part from the beginning as it was important to me that his character didn't seem predatory.

When I first read the script, the moment where they first kiss was electric – a sort of 'oh no, the shit will really hit the fan' – and yet I found myself rooting for them. My judgement was suspended. For me the whole movie is about frailty and human weakness, but also about being non-judgemental. It's about a situation that could be disastrous, and I was trying to defy expectations about that. I liked the idea of this for America because I think the moral majority were always going to leap on the illicit affair for the start, the imbalance of age, and the attack on the family. At the end, the families are breaking up but the film is saying it's OK. We can all progress in our lives without the things we think we need, like family structure. For me this seemed a very modern idea. The idea of family is no longer what it used to be.

Having said all that, were we successful in the movie or not? It got fiercely attacked by many critics, who reviewed it as a drama. People were angry it didn't go to the dark place, but the point of it was not to be dark. That was the reason I liked it but nobody took it as a comedy. We were shocked about how brutal and ferocious some of the reviews were because I thought it was a feel-good movie, frankly! If you look at it in the context of the other romantic comedies I talked about, which are very, very safe, this was the opposite. You could call it a dark premise but it was never a dark movie. It's set in suburbia, not because it's a parody of suburbia but because it's not urban. When I think of urban, I think of it as being darker, more introspective, more brooding and this was the opposite, a freshness of people not overthinking, they were just reacting in the moment, feeling things they weren't in control of. It was subversive in its thinking, but it was a harder one to realise than I expected. There's nothing flash about it, but it deals with real feelings, and people going through painful situations comedically, although there are some scenes without a joke. I thought we should do that with an emotional sincerity. The film was outside the box and suffered for that. There's a much safer place when you do tick the boxes. The actual romance in this had real consequences for other people. The couple had to break up; six months on it was not plausible they would be together. The one thing I felt was most touching was the male friendship; it was tragic that one fell in love with the other's daughter. It was for me about being non-judgemental and allowing people to make mistakes – about human frailty, basically. Which is all quite deep for what is supposed to be a comedy and maybe it is that whole hotchpotch that is an unrealisable one. You'll have to make your own mind up...

CASE STUDY: *HOPE SPRINGS*

Hope Springs is a film that uses the sub-genre of gerontocom. This makes it potentially 'limited' in mass audience appeal – but saying that, because the world population is ageing and in many developed countries one of the core markets (i.e. number of people with disposable income) is men and women in their fifties and above, the film does hit the financial sweet spot. Themes of reinvention and the rekindling of love are prevalent in this and other relationship-orientated films using gerentocom ideas (*The Best Exotic Marigold Hotel*, *Quartet*), where the audience is taken on a heartfelt journey of 'older love' overcoming contemporary world obstacles. For the older audience, who may well have children of their own who are making families and settling down, a film like this not only connects with their life and what might be their situation, but also allows them to revisit their past, now playing out in their children. In this way, a film like *Hope Springs* usefully works with nostalgia and the idea of the 'family unit' to connect with its audience.

The film is a story about how married couple Kay and Arnold attempt to fall back in love after decades of marriage. As might be expected of many longstanding marriages, the passion has gone and the couple are happy to 'plod on' in familiar routines. As they tell their children at the start of the story, for their 31st wedding anniversary they've treated each other to a new cable TV subscription. This clearly sets out, in a world-specific comedic way, the dramatic problem that they face and will have to overcome. As we're told by the film's marketing material, 'the real challenge for both of them comes as they try to re-ignite the spark that caused them to fall for each other in the first place'.

The main spine of the story follows Kay and Arnold as they decide to see a marriage counsellor (aka, sex therapist) who might help them with their problems. Arnold is very reluctant at first, but because we know deep down that he loves Kay more than anything in the world, his decision to go along with it comes as no surprise. This helps to bring a compassionate tone to the story – the situation pulls at our heartstrings because we know this couple is meant to be together forever. Although the flame has died from their marriage, especially sexually, there's no reason to believe that all won't work out in the end. This, of course, also brings an idealistic tone to the story, which is executed in the film's climax.

For the main part of the film, however, a tone of awkwardness prevails – on many levels. Firstly, there's the embarrassment felt by the couple about having to see a counsellor – for Arnold especially. It's like admitting that they can't work things out themselves –worse, they're both in their sixties and the counsellor looks young enough to be their son.

Secondly, the situations Kay and Arnold find themselves in – or, rather, are put in – are awkward and embarrassing – for them and for us! From learning to be 'intimate' with each other again after years in separate beds, to sexual experimentation in a cinema, to 'dressing up' to arouse each other, what we see is pretty cringe-making – but it's also heart-warming and, of course, funny! The advice and tasks provided by the counsellor give a neat structural frame to the story, whereby Kay and Arnold experience progressively more difficult – and awkward – situations.

There's also a third element of tonal awkwardness, and that's related to the casting. Meryl Streep and Tommy Lee Jones are well-known and highly respected actors, and so seeing them in these predominantly sexual situations – and, importantly, at their age – can be very uncomfortable. Again, however, it's still very funny and emotionally uplifting – like any mainstream romantic comedy should be. And as the title promises, hope does spring from their situation, giving a sense of faith for us all!

HOT TIPS

- Know your audience. Imagine how they'll want to relate to your story.

- Get in the habit of reading critics' reviews and then comparing them to box-office statistics.

- Imagine your screenplay (or what you know about it so far) is produced. Write a negative review of it. Now write a glowing review. What does this teach you?

- Ask yourself if commercial success is more important to you than critical acclaim. If you love writing for mainstream audiences, you might be rewarded handsomely with money and bringing audience satisfaction – but develop a thick skin!

GETTING READY TO ROMCOM

In setting out to create and invent a story that deals with the human heart, your characters, their dilemmas and obsessions, and the world they inhabit are bound to be as original as you are an individual. In this sense, you'll be entering and working with the more emotional arenas of your creative mind – putting your unique life stamp into the screenplay and onto the screen. So let's start thinking about where you might get your ideas from, and your process and experience of exploring creatively the whole idea of romance, friendship and identity.

A key thing to remember is that you should try to find an idea that's true to you – unique as a screenplay and something that ultimately reflects your vision and values about the human need for connection. In this case, you might well be experiencing, doing and feeling a lot of other things in the process of creating your unique romcom. These might include:

- Drawing on your own life experiences
- Fantasising about desired life experiences
- Remembering your own lessons in love
- Being emotional on the page where you find it hard in real life
- Confronting your own obstacles to happiness
- Healing your own emotional wounds
- Being inspired by ideas and cultural and social influences
- Blowing your own ideological trumpet
- Exploring something about the human condition
- Making a comment about relationships and social attitudes today

A good way to start is to think about the uniqueness of you, the screenwriter, and your own take on love, happiness and human connection.

VALUES

On one level, you'll always be unconsciously or consciously processing 'the times', particularly values and attitudes to do with love, family, marriage, partnership and intimacy. As writers, the stories we create can't help but be informed and influenced by the world around us – social mores, cultural expectations, etc. – but they're always ultimately skewed by our individual and unique perspectives, and by our values system.

For example, gay rights are most clearly in flux when it comes to the right for LGBT people to get married. As countries deal with legislation in different ways, it becomes a focus in the media. It also uniquely affects individuals on a very personal level as they try to protect their love and commitment to each other from changes and inconsistency in the law. At the time of writing this book, there's certainly a rise in LGBT characters (if not protagonists) in different genres (such as *A Single Man*, *Blue is the Warmest Colour*, *I Love You Phillip Morris*) – so clearly, as writers, we're being inspired by the increased focus in (predominantly) Western society on 'gay rights'. We're also perhaps inspired by – or angry about – what we feel is oppressive and unequal in other cultures.

....

EXERCISE – THE VALUES SYSTEM OF YOUR ROMCOM

This exercise is intended to get you thinking about your own values system, and how it might inform your writing. Answer the following questions and try to be spontaneous – write the first thing that comes into your mind.

1. What do humans need from other humans to function well?

2. Did your parents or carers approve or disapprove of any relationships you had when you were growing up? What were their reasons for this? Did you agree then? Do you agree now?

3. What do you think of the concept of Valentine's Day?

4. Do you believe anyone has the right to choose (and marry) whomever they love? What do you feel are the restrictions?

5. Do you believe everyone has the right to marriage?

6. Why do we need romantic comedy stories?

7. What is wrong with the romantic comedies that you don't like?

8. Whose love stories don't get enough screen time? Why don't they?

....

VISION

The entrepreneurs behind start-up companies often ask similar questions in early brainstorms of their motivation, their market and finding a way towards a Unique Selling Point. This kind of approach can be useful for the screenwriter, too. What you write here (particularly if you haven't begun your project) can form a useful core vision and values statement about a potential romcom. It can also be useful to refer back to during later stages of development, to remind you where your project came from and what it was supposed to be about.

....

EXERCISE - THE VISION

Ask yourself the following questions in order to understand your vision:

1. Why do I want to write this romcom?

2. Who would really enjoy my story? What is the personality type of someone who would 'get' it?

3. Why is my romcom unique?

4. What are my favourite types of romcom?

5. What romcom characters/situations have I never seen?

6. What romcom character has given me the most pleasure? Why?

Keep your answers handy so you can come back to them later, once you've entered the development process and need to refocus on what story you're actually trying to tell.

EMOTIONAL TERRITORY

You can't write a romcom without embracing emotion, so, as the song goes, show some! If you aren't a particularly emotionally expressive person, you might be fantastically expressive on the page. Perhaps writing a romcom is actually your way of showing emotion. A really emotionally expressive writer in real life doesn't guarantee success in the genre, but it might help. We'll be talking about the important element of comedic tone later, but for now think about how choosing a tone might be the result of your own individual 'taste' regarding the expression of emotions. See these emotional arenas as helpful and fertile sources for the originality of your romcom, particularly the characters and their dilemmas – which, as with any screenplay, lie at the heart of the story.

EXERCISE – SHOW SOME EMOTION

Here are some more questions targeted at helping you understand your attitudes and values towards emotion. Answer them honestly and thoroughly!

1. Define 'happiness'. What do you think makes people happy today, in your world, according to your definition? What stops people from being happy?

2. Do you consider yourself to be happy?

3. Are you in love? Have you ever been? When? What did it feel like?

4. Do you feel 'loved' in general? By whom, and how? If not, why do you think you are unloved?

5. Do you consider yourself lucky or unlucky in love? Why?

6. What's the biggest issue that comes up for you in intimate relationships?

7. Have you ever been heartbroken? How did you get through it? Who helped you?

8. What's the most romantic thing you've ever done?

9. What's the most unromantic thing you've done?

Hopefully these questions don't trigger too much of an uncomfortable trip down Memory Lane! The main point is to get you thinking and feeling about your own personal experiences of happiness, love, connection, romance and intimacy. With any luck you may have gained some new perspectives – or just got yourself into the emotional territory that writing a romcom will inevitably lead you to.

QUICK **INSIGHT**

Suya Lee, a Melbourne-based writer and PhD student researching comedy and farce in screenwriting.

Sadie Hawkins says forget leap year, try today instead!

Let's imagine reversing the traditional marriage proposal that we see all too often in romantic comedies...

Ladies first. Would you ask a guy to marry you? I dare you to step into the man's shoes – plus a little extra.

You want this proposal to be both romantic and perfect. You've been suckered into the marketing ploys of saving three months' salary for the right engagement ring. You've booked his favourite restaurant on your anniversary, plus his special table by the fireplace. And you've arranged with the manager to play his favourite song just as the desserts are served. You've spent the entire day getting ready for this one big moment, and splurged plenty. You've gotten your hair just right, a facial to perfect your glow, a pedi and a mani to match your red-hot sexy number, bought new shoes and had a fresh Brazilian wax.

Both of you order your respective favourite dishes and you've pre-ordered his dream champagne, just to make the whole ordeal go down more smoothly. Your boyfriend digs into the cheesecake. You get up, straighten your dress and get on one knee to propose. You make sure that your mini dress doesn't ride up your ass – or worse. You say the precious four words, 'Will you marry me?', as you open the small box.

Gentlemen next. How would you feel about a woman proposing to you on bended knee?

You think she's finally asked you out to dinner, meaning that she will pay. You think she's gone all out with the steak and lobster, not to mention the champagne. You don't notice the playlist that's been blasting over the restaurant. You notice she's stood up and think she's heading to the restroom. She's fallen on one knee – you should help her get up, but you stare at her boobs hanging out of her low cleavage. She's just said something weird, and then showed you some shiny gold stuff that's distracted you from looking at her chest. Hang on... she's just proposed! The entire restaurant claps. What's she doing? You don't even live together. Do you run, laugh or pretend not to hear her? Instead, you choke on the cheesecake.

Since biblical times, there's been the odd story of a woman proposing to a man. Why not more, ladies? Don't want to seem desperate? Think it's too bold? How about feeling un-feminine? Does it take guts to get down on your stilettos to ask a man for his hand? Isn't this the 21st century? How about challenging the status quo... again? The screwball comedies of the 1930s and 1940s, such as *Bringing Up Baby*, bucked the status quo – but it didn't last. How about challenging your romcom story in this day and age?

EXERCISE – A ROMANTIC INTERLUDE

The purpose of this exercise is to give your inner artist a romantic treat! We can ignore our own needs for pleasure and escapism, but then expect ourselves to be able to churn romantic experiences and characters' enjoyment of these out onto the page. As most romantic comedies emphasise the need for self-love before you can love anybody else, you need to make sure that you're actually treating yourself well!

Treat yourself for one day to a conventionally romantic experience on your own. Imagine what you would really love your partner or fantasy partner to do for you, to woo you and make you feel cherished. For example, breakfast in bed, a red rose on your desk, love songs, a candlelit dinner, etc. Alternatively, if you find conventional romance simply horrendous, try to work out the more appealing and non-conventional ways of being romantic with which to treat yourself. For example, the red rose can be wild flowers sourced from a country walk.

After the event, brainstorm in a written list all of the sensations and emotions you experienced. Then ask yourself:

How would another person make it better?
How would creating the experience for another person feel?

Hopefully the idea of this exercise isn't too cringe-making! Have a go. Many writers can be quite self-denying, but for those of you who have no problem in treating yourself regularly, to music, art, flowers and great experiences, try to think about something you wouldn't normally do. The whole point of this exercise is to feel and sense new experiences and emotions related to romance.

....

FINDING THE IDEA FOR YOUR SCREENPLAY

We've spoken quite a lot about ideas so far, and our approach to the book through *ideation*. But how do you actually find an idea for a romcom? Where do you start – and how do you know when you've started? Before we give you some specific pointers for finding ideas, let's talk about ideas themselves.

Ideas for screenplays come from both outside and inside of us. As screenwriters we constantly think about what's happening around us (socially, culturally, economically, politically), and what's happening within us (emotionally, psychologically). When we put these two things together – processing events happening around you into internal thoughts and feelings – we get theme and meaning. And then when we put all of this into screenplay form, we get storytelling. And that's why we love stories: because they tell us about the world we live in, and through a lens we understand (the human perspective). Our view on or interpretation of the world is different to the next person's – and that's what makes unique and refreshing stories.

In terms of the romcom, your views, interpretations – and experiences – of love, romance and sex are bound to be 'different' in some way, and that difference is what an audience is seeking out. Although they probably won't meet or even know what the screenwriter looks like, an audience desperately wants to hear their ideas. You have ideas – and so your audience needs you!

As we'll outline below, story ideas come from a multitude of places and experiences, many of them specific to you and your life. The main thing to say here is that whenever you see, hear or *feel* a story, keep it tucked away somewhere to use later. You might come back to it another day, either as the starting point for a new story or to inject into a screenplay you're already writing. You might also find yourself being asked for your next idea – by a producer, for example – so it's good to have a bank of ideas somewhere.

IDEATION

An idea is only an idea when it's got a future – when it's got the potential to go somewhere. Otherwise, it's just a fact – just a 'thing'. An idea suggests intention – something that resides in the 'thing' that's got the potential to become something else. In the case of a romcom, it's a musing about a character or a plot or a theme or a world that will eventually become a funny and heart-warming screenplay. Because our ideas are intended for other people, they need to have something that's going to interest and connect with them. Sometimes this is clear from the start. At other times, it's going to take the advice of someone in the development process to help you. Either way, your idea needs to have some appealing qualities that will warrant the film being made. A crucial thing to consider here is its universal appeal. What's in your idea that others will want to hear about, and possibly share? How will your romcom create an emotional connection with its intended audience?

This is where it's useful to ask, what's in the zeitgeist? What are people talking about at the minute? What are society's concerns? These are useful questions to ask because you're trying to reach out to people's emotions and get them to feel what you're trying to say. What's being explored in your story might not necessarily tap into the specific consciousness of the people you're writing for – though it should certainly tap into their emotions – but it should tap into the consciousness of the people you're writing about. Films can easily fall down because they don't feel relevant to the characters' world.

For example, Australian romcom *Any Questions for Ben* feels really inappropriate for its characters. The film explores ideas of self-worth, social value and missed chances – all of which would suit a mid-life-crisis type of situation. But the protagonist, Ben, is 27, and practically all of his friends are around the same age. What's worse is that Ben declares his love for Alex, telling her that he regrets never getting to know her at university, and how he remembers watching her in the canteen in-between lectures, and how he was enamoured of her. But because at 27 he's likely to have left university only five or six years before, it feels contrived and convenient rather than credible and true. If the central characters had been shaped around the film's core themes, making the world of the story much more believable, the film might have been much more successful – critically and commercially. That's why it's really important when developing an idea to allow time for the story to find a shape and a voice that speaks to its characters.

The more you let an idea gestate, the stronger it's likely to be. Sometimes we make quick judgements and decisions, but it's only when we let them brew for a while and come back to them that they find their own way. In screenwriting, this makes the film feel more original and true. If you let an idea breathe and morph, you'll probably be happier with what you're writing.

It can also be useful to read how other writers find and develop their ideas. Although everyone works differently, there are common themes – recognising when an idea's good, first steps to developing that idea, probing and expanding the idea, knowing when the idea's running out of steam, etc. Graeme Harper's book, *Inside Creative Writing: Interviews with Contemporary Writers* (2012), asks a host of practising writers about the processes they go through when writing creatively. A book like this can be insightful and inspiring. Kevin Conroy Scott's *Screenwriters' Masterclass* (2005) and Alistair Owen's *Story and Character* (2004) offer a range of interviews with well-credited screenwriters, and are really useful for understanding how writers work.

INSPIRATION

Idea inspiration can come in many forms and from many sources. Here we'll outline just a few sources of motivation for your screenplay.

THE LIGHT BULB MOMENT

You're on the train gazing out the window; you're in the shower; you're taking a walk; or you're doing the ironing. Then, ping! Out of some dark hemisphere of the brain comes the most brilliant of ideas. You rush to your pen and paper or voice memo and get the idea down. It might just be a character – someone you've never seen before, someone so delightfully or crazily unique that you experience something like love at first sight.

Or you might have an idea for a plot. Or you might have a strong feeling for theme. In this situation, two things can happen – either you get down to it and write, or, as with most of us, life takes over. The idea will still be there, but days pass. Or in some cases weeks... months... years! But something about the idea endures. Aspects of the story might begin to feel dated and will need adjusting, and similar films might come and go, but you feel your story is still original and deserves to find an audience.

ARTISTIC ADMIRATION

The romcoms and dramedies of Diablo Cody (*Juno*, *Young Adult*), Julie Delpy (*Before Sunset*, *Before Sunrise*, *Before Midnight*), Nancy Meyers (*Something's Gotta Give*, *The Holiday*, *It's Complicated*) or Woody Allen (*Annie Hall*, *Vicky Cristina Barcelona*) might have great aesthetic resonance for you in how they approach love and comedy. In other words, you're a fan and you want to write like them. Rather, you consciously want to write something similar and potentially as successful, but with your own distinctive take on character and story. Writing that's borne out of admiration is a very different creature to that which is just a pale imitation. If you break down the elements of what you admire in a writer or director's work (e.g. tone, style, theme, characterisation, etc.) and why you admire it, you can apply these qualities to your own original writing.

YOUR LIFE

In the context of screenplay ideas, there might be a specific relationship you've personally experienced that triggers the need for resolution through writing. Perhaps you have a need for vengeance as you feel betrayed? For mourning the loss of love? Or for celebrating finding 'the one'? Perhaps you still long for 'the one' and writing a screenplay is a way of filling that void. In *Ruby Sparks* a lonely and emotionally remote writer does exactly that as he simply can't attract the right kind of woman.

Sometimes emotional wounds can last a long time, and are so deeply buried we don't know we're carrying them around with us. They're part of our unconscious and come alive in dreams and fantasies, and affect how we relate to others. As suggested above, for writers emotional wounds can be the underlying layer for a story idea. It's kind of obvious therefore that romantic comedy is an ideal genre for characters that need to work out emotional issues that keep getting in the way of love. Only you can say if you're choosing romantic comedy – in its broadest definition – to explore, if not heal, some of your own heartache, and also to what extent your main characters reflect your own emotional pains or relationship patterns. The character of Shakespeare in classic bioromcom *Shakespeare in Love* needed to feel love, pain and loss before he could access his inner muse.

....

EXERCISE – WHERE ARE YOU AT?

This exercise encourages you to define where you are at emotionally, at the time of deciding to write a romcom. Read the following statements and see which might reflect 'where you are at'.

- I feel disillusioned with life and love.
- I want to escape banality and routine – I want romance!
- I like formulaic and predictable funny stories that are what they say on the tin.
- I wish I could find the perfect partner. I get close, but there's something always wrong with them.
- I've found Mr/Mrs Right. Now I want to explore what happens after the happy ending!
- I feel like a loser, a weird freak who can't relate to people.
- I believe there is somebody for everybody. Maybe somebodies!
- I believe in happy endings.
- I'm happy in love and I want everybody else to feel as good as me.
- I want marriage and kids and will feel my life is a failure if I don't get them.
- Relationships suck.
- I don't believe people should have to change. If someone gets you, isn't that enough?

Wherever you are at, this place will inevitably be part of your motivation to write a romcom. In particular, it will influence your themes and messages – happy or sad!

There's nothing wrong with being too close to home in subject matter, so long as you can remain objective in terms of what'll work as a film, and can find ways of making it interesting and relevant to others, not just yourself. Another important point to remember is that if you're using the screenplay as 'emotional payback' – to make yourself feel better in terms of retaliation – it might not be emotionally well balanced. The sour feelings you have might leave a sour taste in your audience's mouth – which often isn't a good thing. Personal responsibility – 'it takes two to tango' – and forgiveness of the self and others are central ingredients of many successful romantic comedies, and especially to the 'feel-good' buzz in an up-ending love story.

Having said that, *Forgetting Sarah Marshall* is a good example of the 'retaliatory romcom', in which the protagonist just needs to get over being treated really badly by a cheating ex before he can move on (while she ends up with the deserved fate of being sad and alone).

THE GREAT IDEA

Finding an idea that you feel will speak to many people's experience of love, but which hasn't been 'done' – or done with your unique voice and vision – could be your original motivation. Similar to the Light Bulb Moment, the Great Idea is more of a considered and rational approach. It can come as a result of creative brainstorming between a writer and a director, or a writer and a producer. It might be a helpful friend who has a Great Idea and gives it to you because they know they're not a writer. Very often, the Great Idea supplied by others is based on some of their own crazy or memorable experiences in relationships. They might have been dumped by text or tweet. They had a weird meet as opposed to a 'meet cute'. Then the usual 'rules' apply – only convincing characters, not ones just based on your friend or colleague, will pull it off. If the Great Idea comes to you alone, then it's a good idea to test it out with friends. Other people, and the films they know about, can be surprisingly helpful in ensuring your Great Idea hasn't been done already.

HIGH-CONCEPT

You might find an amazing 'high-concept' idea that springs from the zeitgeist or from a 'what if?' brainstorming session. A high-concept romcom is one where the external situation facing the character is almost as dramatically intriguing and important as the character themselves. Situations can be high-stakes or conflict-ridden, or just plain funny. There's generally an element of dramatic irony in the mix. *The Change Up* is a good example, where two men swap bodies as the result of a lightning strike. The sexually active bachelor Mitch takes the form of the happily married Dave, who finds himself in Mitch's body. With funny results, lightning legitimises Dave's newfound freedom, while Mitch learns the qualities of commitment through being married.

Another example of high-concept is the film *It's Complicated*, another 'retaliatory romcom' in which a divorced middle-aged woman has a secret affair with her ex-husband, thereby gaining some revenge in the process on both her ex and his younger lover. The affair gives the character closure and helps her to move on and find new love. It also manages to ensure her husband is the 'ultimate loser' in that he turns out to be single, alone and without a family – the children pretty much take their mother's side. The comedic triumph of the dumped middle-aged woman adds to the intrigue of the high-concept situation.

FINDING THE TITLE

Finding the perfect title for a romcom is a bit like finding the perfect partner – you can strike lucky first time around, or you'll go through a laborious process of trial and mainly error until you find 'the one'. In general, titles for romcoms tend to be:

SHORT

Short and snappy tends to be more memorable. You can't get shorter than *Ted* – a film about a teddy bear, but *There's Something About Mary* and *Eternal Sunshine of the Spotless Mind* are great examples of titles that flout the rules. On the whole, using a character's name is easy, and tends to be the fall-back position for biopics or dramas. But, then again, there's always an exception, such as the romcom *Annie Hall*, which won an Oscar for Best Original Screenplay. *Forgetting Sarah Marshall*, *Kissing Jessica Stein*, and *Along Came Polly* suggest to the audience the life-changing magnitude and importance of the loved one or ex. *Notting Hill* conjures up the iconic London area in which the film is set, and it also happens to be very much a Notting Hill type of love – a superstar who can afford to live there, and an eccentric, floppy-haired bookseller.

LITERAL

These types of title tend to say exactly what the film is, which might link well to the premise it's being sold on. *Four Christmases*, for example, is about exactly that. The content is certainly what it says on the tin.

METAPHORICAL

A literal title can also be a metaphorical one, where the title suggests a deeper meaning that might emerge before or after seeing the film. *Four Christmases* raises an eyebrow as we normally go 'somewhere', i.e. one place, for Christmas. The fact that this is going to be about four Christmases immediately tells us that things are going to be complicated. *The Holiday* is about a holiday, a break from the routine of life. In the case of its heroines, this holiday changes their lives forever.

Austenland is another example of a metaphorical title. It's witty in itself – there's no such place but it does sound like a country. Yes, it's a Jane Austen theme park, so it's literal, but it also suggests a mindset of the crazy fandom surrounding Jane Austen. The fact that the film is about Americans obsessed with anything and everything related to Jane Austen, and a particular version of British culture, is also indicated in the title.

The notion of baggage – a character's baggage – in the title neatly conjures up ideas of unresolved emotional wounds that are going to get in the way of love. An example of this is *Baggage Claim*.

ARCHETYPAL

Many film titles have something that conjures up a well-known if not universal element of the story or premise. *Bad Teacher* invokes the familiar archetype that most of us have encountered – a teacher that has failed us or him or herself in their educational role. *Young Adult* is a stage we've all been at – a rites of passage to maturity, and as a film title it also hints at arrested development, which is certainly the case with protagonist Mavis.

The archetypal nature of the title can also be a well-known expression, such as *Something's Gotta Give* or *Whatever Works*. On one level these are conversational generalisations, but on the other hand they're truisms that make sense in the context of the minefield of modern relationships.

IRONIC

The Five-Year Engagement is ironic in itself. It suggests that problems and obstacles beset the days from the proposal/decision to marry right through to the wedding day. *Four Weddings and a Funeral* reveals a dramedic quality, though as a joke in itself we know the film isn't going to be too sombre. *Bridesmaids* suggests sisterhood, dresses, cakes and hen parties. The film flips the idealised feminine dream on its head with extreme irreverence.

INDICATIVE OF GENRE

Romantic comedy titles mainly have a tonal quality that suggests the film is lighter and deals with romance, such as *Wedding Crashers* and *What's Your Number?* On the contrary, dramatic romance *Autumn in New York* hasn't got much that's amusing about it, nor any irony. With this title we might instead think of the looming bleakness of winter, the seasons of life, and the romantic elements of New York in late Autumn – fitting for a love story about a dying girl.

. . . .

EXERCISE – FINDING A TITLE

Nobody can come up with anything good when sitting at a desk, staring at the wall or even out of the window. This is a fun and unpredictable, 'free yet contrived association' exercise to nudge you to think outside the box when it comes to titles. Don't try to be clever, or overthink it. There are really no right or wrong answers!

Cut up lots of small pieces of paper. On each one, write the answers to the following brainstorms or questions, and put them in the respective jars, or just piles, folded up. Try to put one word on each piece of paper.

Jar One

1. If your screenplay were a flower, what type would it be? Why?
2. If your screenplay were an animal, what type would it be? Why?
3. If your screenplay were a car, what type would it be? Why?
4. If your screenplay were a colour, what would it be? And what tone?
5. If your screenplay were a mood, what would it be?

Jar Two

6. Brainstorm some adjectives that describe your character's attitude to life.
7. Brainstorm some adjectives that describe your character's emotional past and ongoing problems or issues.
8. Find some lyrics that could reflect the main character's ongoing problem.
9. Brainstorm the location your screenplay is set. Limit yourself to adjectives to describe the world.
10. Brainstorm all the emotions that your screenplay could evoke.

Shake both jars and start selecting from each jar to form phrases. Remember, it doesn't matter if they don't make sense! Write these down and see if any trigger some interesting thoughts on titles.

....

CASE STUDY: *VALENTINE'S DAY*

VALUES

Valentine's Day is an ensemble romantic dramedy set over one day in Los Angeles. Its large, star-studded cast leads the multiple storylines of characters making their way through the day and dealing with the emotional situations of their love lives. Because Valentine's Day is traditionally the most romantic day of the year, what this special day means for the characters, and how the day itself is a catalyst for solving matters of the heart, provides the 'engine' of the film.

For screenwriters who aspire to write studio-style mainstream films for a large worldwide audience, *Valentine's Day* is a good example of the ingredients required for a successful, mainstream romcom. The film was followed by *New Year's Eve*, another highly successful romcom.

VISION

Valentine's Day is a traditionally romantic, feel-good and easy-going film. It's the ultimate date night movie. LA looks beautiful – the sun is always shining and the spirit of romance is everywhere. The actors that have been cast are supremely attractive. Being happy in love, finding your soulmate and going the distance for the right partner are the romantic ideas forming most of the storylines. The messages that emotional truth is important, knowing yourself will lead to happiness, and having the courage to communicate your needs are emphasised by the happy resolutions of the multiple storylines. The vision recreates the fairy tale of happy-ever-after, and lives that are probably very different to those of most of the audience.

In other words, the 'vision' of *Valentine's Day* can be seen as making a promise to deliver big on the feel-good factor for audiences who like upbeat, emotional and sentimental films. And there's nothing wrong with that!

AUDIENCE

Valentine's Day successfully appealed to a big and broad audience of viewers. It offered moviegoers an escape into feel-good and positive messages. Worldwide box-office takings were over $200,000,000. The core audience was probably women, who are typically the main 'consumers' of the romantic comedy. In terms of age, the audience could be anywhere between 15 and 50 – but that's not to exclude young girls or boys who might fancy Ashton Kutcher, older people who love escapism and romance, and fans of Julia Roberts. The point is that *Valentine's Day* achieved its objective to gain massive commercial success, have huge internal reach, and provide its audience with a feel-good Hollywood experience.

CRITICS

Critics' reactions to *Valentine's Day* were extremely negative. The website www.rottentomatoes.com gives the film only 18% on the tomatometer, with a fairly disparaging overview: 'Eager to please and stuffed with stars, *Valentine's Day* squanders its promise with a frantic, episodic plot and an abundance of rom-com clichés.'

When looking at individual extracts from critics, the biggest issues cited seem to revolve around the emotional subject matter and the perfect world – in other words, the exact 'vision' the film was trying to promote. Box-office statistics clearly conflict with this negative perspective, showing that *Valentine's Day* didn't please all people all the time, but it did deliver on its vision's promise to its audience.

TITLE

The title says it all. Simple, evocative, known the world over and hasn't been done (at least in the recent past).

HOT TIPS

- Know 'what' your story is: work out its vision and values about love and romance.

- Create a 'mood board' with images that convey the emotions your story will evoke in its audience.

- Rate the different 'audiences' in terms of priority. Whose opinion do you really care about? Why?

- Choose one produced film that reflects your own version of happiness in love. Say why this is, in one sentence. Print out that sentence and stick it near your writing area as a constant reminder of what you're trying to achieve.

A FUNNY KIND OF LOVE

What kind of romantic comedian are you? Are you gushing? Sentimental? Cynical? Gross-out? Or downright dark, bitter and twisted, someone whose idea of a fulfilling romantic comedy is a really nasty end for anyone who's rejected you?

Probably the most difficult thing to know when starting out is the comedic tone your story should take, particularly if you've never tried to write a romantic comedy before. You might be worried that the tone you establish just won't be funny. Or that you're not a gag writer. Or that the audience just won't get it.

On one level, you're right to be worried. Declaring to the world you're writing any kind of comedy implies you think you're funny, and you could be setting yourself up to fail big time if nobody laughs. Just like the horror that isn't scary, or the tragic drama that makes people collapse in a fit of giggles. But what's funny to you might not be funny to your girlfriend or boyfriend, let alone the next-door neighbour.

Now put that into the context of development. What's funny to the script editor or producer might not be funny to you, or vice versa. Simpatico chemistry is an essential requirement of the development process of a romantic comedy. Sometimes you can watch something that makes other people laugh, but you sit still, stony-faced, perplexed that anyone can smile at scenes that to you aren't remotely amusing. The point is, comedic tone is a fragile and unique thing.

Tone is important for many reasons, but it's a frequently ignored element when we watch or talk about romantic comedies from the perspective of the audience. Tone can also be overlooked when thinking about the art and craft of writing a screenplay. However, a good writer or reader will know when the tone jars, feels off-kilter, or is inconsistent and just doesn't work. The biggest challenge to writers is to get down on the page a successful range of comedic tones that work for your story, normally with one more dominant over the others. Your ultimate aim is to get the screenplay's first audience – the reader – to *see* and *feel* the potential film, and for them to laugh where you intend it – and, if possible, elsewhere!

Watching romantic comedies from other cultures can be enlightening with regard to the incredible range of tones available. Just like with individuals and social groups, what's funny to one culture might be irritating – even offensive – to another. That comedy doesn't travel or age well is a mixed maxim. Some do, and some don't. The 1980 film *A Fish Called Wanda* is the most hilarious romcom to some – even if it wasn't marketed as a romcom – while a younger audience might find it dumb. A 1950s bromcom/capercom/romcom like *Some Like It Hot* has stood the test of time better, entertaining generation after generation. So if there's a comedic X-factor that ages well, hope and pray that your specific tone has it!

The good news is that, unless you really are deeply dark, bitter and twisted, you should be able to find a romantic comedic tone that you're comfortable writing, that suits the characters, world and themes of your story, and, at a broader level, ticks the box for the upbeat and feel-good humour that an audience of any romcom requires.

For all the planning and storytelling you involve yourself in, your inherent comedic tone will emerge when you actually begin the screenplay, writing the action and giving voice to your characters. But before then it can be helpful to try to work out what you'd like to achieve through tone – and why.

TYPES OF COMEDY FOUND IN THE ROMCOM

Romantic comedies tend to employ several comedic tones and comic devices as a way of expressing their stories and finding their audiences. Using the hugely successful dramedy chumcom/romcom *Bridemaids* as an example, let's look at how different types of comedy are woven into a narrative through characters, situations, dynamics and events, to create 'tonal tapestry'.

Satire pokes fun. Think of satire as the person who's a compulsive and derisive mocker, if a subtle one. It's the person who wants to bring everyone down to size with witty yet cutting comments. In a way satire is very equalising, taking no prisoners. In romantic comedy, satire is often created in the characters' compulsive and unresolved approaches to love. In *Bridesmaids*, satire is overtly used with love rat Ted and rival maid of honour Helen. Protagonist Annie does not escape either, as the opening scene shows her going to great lengths to look beautiful first thing, which is a huge act of contrivance. It's even more funny that Ted only wants her for sex anyway.

Farce is just plain silly, normally with a big dollop of unlikely chaos thrown into the mix. It's funny because it goes against the grain of reason and what could be remotely sensible. In *Bridesmaids*, moments of farce underlie the end of the opening sequence, where Annie tries to leave Ted's luxury pad of with dignity but can't actually open the electronic gate. To avoid calling him, she decides to climb over the gate. Mid-straddle, the gate rolls wide open with Annie astride on top. Any semblance of dignity is thrown back in her face by the farcical situation she finds herself in, and to add insult to injury Ted is probably watching with great mirth. Because the film doesn't ever give his POV we're spared this, but the face of a couple watching from a car says enough. Later, on the plane to Vegas, Annie is extremely affected by tranquillisers and alcohol, leading to very silly behaviour that results in the women being asked to leave the plane when it arrives.

Somewhere between satire and farce is *ridicule*. There's something ridiculous about the low self-esteem of Annie and the antics it produces. Rival maid of honour Helen's extreme competitiveness and need to crush Annie's pathetic attempts also border on farce.

Gross-out, physical comedy makes us cringe and howl in revulsion. Bodily control is a 'norm' of society, so falling foul of the norm in very traditional situations causes the audience to identify in shame. In the bridal dress shop, the *Bridesmaids* women are having a fitting when their earlier dodgy Mexican lunch bites back with a vengeance, causing the lovely ladies to surrender to vomiting and diarrhoea all over the shop. Hardly romantic! It's an iconic scene, a first to blend scatological humour with women and weddings!

A *dramedic* tone adds the required emotional intensity to a romantic comedy. It asks the audience to empathise and relate to the unresolved wounds in the protagonist, and to actively care about resolution of these problems and difficulties, so it can be described as having an empathic quality. It helps us 'buy into' the character, and gun for them. Pure farce, in sharp contrast, would have the opposite effect of distancing us. Annie's self-pity and low self-esteem cause plenty of dramedic moments, where pathos and pain are more sensitively drawn. Seeing her failed cupcake shop boarded up, for instance. Going home to live with her mother, who's bitter and unresolved over her ex-husband's new relationship, is humiliating for a late-thirty-something woman.

While the bitter mother can be a familiar 'type' in female-driven romantic comedies, somehow symbolising what could become of a woman who doesn't work on her anger with men, Annie also shows great tenderness to her mother as her dented self-esteem recovers. Likewise, when Megan visits Annie at her lowest point, and shares her own private hell of being bullied at school and dealing with it, the connection between the women is mainly dramedic with some robust physical comedy thrown in – Megan punches Annie repeatedly to make her see what she's doing to herself. When protagonists finally 'make good' on their destructive behaviour, and take responsibility for their problems, these scenes are usually written with a dramedic tone.

The *romantic tone* is essential to the romantic comedy in all its forms, platonic or sexual. Does romantic love have to be sexual? In *Bridesmaids*, Annie behaves like a jilted lover who uses the excuse of rejection by a loved one to avoid looking at the deeper problems she faces, like low self-esteem, failure and masochistic relationships. She literally pines for her friend. There's absolutely no sense of romance between Annie and Ted, compared to the later heartbreak and yearning she feels for Rhodes. Annie identifies as straight, but clearly doesn't get any sexual satisfaction with Ted. She's intimacy avoidant, except with Rhodes. Audiences expect moments that reflect the emotional pleasure of togetherness and love, and while most mainstream romantic comedies avoid bisexual physical impulses in their protagonists, the romance of platonic love is alive and kicking. There's almost a sexual tension between Annie and Lillian. On a purely romantic level, Annie leaving a carrot cake outside the house of rejected and hurt traffic cop Rhodes is romantic, when we see the effort she's put into it. It's made funny when she drives back a few days later to see it eaten by wild animals.

Joyousness is the ultimate feel-good tone of romantic comedies, one that usually dominates the end of the film, following the Act Three climax. This guarantees the audience will leave with smiles on their faces. The joyous tone is also the tone responsible for cringe-making elements of a romantic comedy. Joyous tones reflect the human need for unity and coming together, and the healing power of great happiness. As a writer, you'll either love it or hate it. You can treat it as a big serving of candyfloss that you're forced to eat, or that you happily gobble up like manna from heaven. The performance by the women for their newly married friend at the end of *Bridesmaids* is pure unadulterated joy and bliss – the ultimate send-off. And it's here that irreverent tones of satire can still creep in, subtly distilling the in-your-face sensation of total joy and love.

QUICK **INSIGHT**

Bump and tangle
Suya Lee

In real life, before the cellphone (circa 1973), you'd generally avoid bumping into other people by not paying attention, especially on the street and on public transport. These days, distracted people can go one step further and get tangled up with other people – items such as bag straps, scarves and umbrellas. People are also increasingly getting tangled up – which for screenplays can be comedy gold.

We think that bumping into each other and getting tangled up is a lovely way for two people to meet in our stories, hoping that they'll fall in love at first sight. You might increase the impact by making them get tangled up closer as they try to untangle themselves from each other. Just look at all the stories that use this little but weighted story device. Or you could turn this around – the two people bump into each other and it's hate at first sight. If this is the case, tangle them up more to increase their annoyance and irritability, so that the characters have to work harder to fall in love as the story progresses. Make your characters work for their love! An audience wants its money's worth, after all...

DEVELOPING YOUR ROMANTIC COMEDY TONE

Tone and writing practice is a bit like muscle tone and exercise. The more you practise, the stronger you get. Just like the effects of working out on your body, your comic tone becomes evident on the page but is always affected by the raw material – your comic DNA, if you like. In other words, as a writer, how you use tone is as distinctive and unique as you are as a person. It'll inevitably reflect your values, attitudes, choices and tastes – and these are yours alone. Tone is influenced by your:

- Culture
- Gender
- Socio-economic status
- Psychology
- World view
- Personality
- Mood at the time of writing
- Writing voice

What makes a unique and distinctive romcom writer is the unique combination of all these factors. The romantic comedies of Billy Wilder, Woody Allen, Judd Apatow, Julie Delpy, Nancy Meyers and Diablo Cody are all unique and distinctive not just because of recurrent themes and ideas, approaches to characterisation and worlds and settings that we find in their work, but also because of their distinctive uses of tone.

....

EXERCISE – WHATEVER WORKS

Firstly, choose one of your favourite contemporary romantic comedies. Watch the film armed with a pen and pad, and make a note of when you laugh or smile with happiness (i.e. any feel-good inspired response). Analyse the whole film scene by scene in this way, trying to identify the main comedic tones listed above. Pay particular attention to what's happening to the protagonist(s) when you have happy reactions. Work out why it works for you.

Secondly, choose a much older romantic comedy – at least three decades old. It could be a 1970s Woody Allen, a 1950s Doris Day, or a 1930s screwball. Repeat the above and pay particular attention to what's still funny. What seems dated in terms of humour? How and why – cringe-making, old-fashioned, or plain old offensive?

....

TONE AS EMOTIONAL PARADIGM

Another way you can develop your skills in creating different comedic tones is to think about tone in terms of its emotional effects. In this way, rather than thinking about tones as satirical or dramedic, for example, you'll be thinking of them in terms of the feelings they can generate in an audience, and that motivate you in the writing process (hopefully you'll feel them when writing!).

We've come up with the following main categories for 'tone as emotion' when writing a romantic comedy, which we'll look at in more detail.

- The Tone of *Anger*
- The Tone of *Awkwardness*
- The Tone of *Compassion*
- The Tone of *Idealism*

THE TONE OF ANGER

To describe anger as a tone in romantic comedy sounds rather incongruous, but really it's a way of thinking about the mirth you want to create in your audience from the characters' misfortunes in relationships – *because they deserve it* somehow, or because *life isn't fair* – and you, the writer, are angry about it on some level. If you use the tone of anger, you have to actively enjoy writing about one character being humiliated, either by their own stupidity, by someone else or by society's double standards. In other words, all those moments of excruciating pain, humiliation, betrayal, extreme power, greed, the compulsive need to win, puerile teasing, goading, mocking, belittling, the desire for getting even and the drive for vengeance create an underlying tone of anger.

As a writer of this tone, you enjoy creating (and probably watching) the merriment created by the abuse of power that all too frequently occurs in human relationships and society. An angry tone can stem from a heavily disguised misanthropic attitude that capitalises on the more ego-driven aspects of relating to others. It's a very divisive tone in its own right but, woven into your narrative with skill, it can be very funny. It can be puerile, immature, shallow and vindictive when one character is clearly the 'bad guy', or Mr or Ms Wrong. Physical comedy often has an angry undercurrent to it. Anger is essentially a reaction to unfair or hurtful treatment, and so creating characters that deal out or receive bad treatment will generate a sense of anger in the audience. In the romantic comedy, that anger can be diffused in different ways.

Firstly, it's diffused through the protagonist as victim in 'retaliatory romcoms'. As we've seen, the long-suffering protagonist can sometimes attract cruelty from secondary characters – almost as if they're asking for it unless they change. Their nasty behaviour finds a willing recipient in the masochistic nature of the protagonist. Examples include Stu's vindictive and control-freak wife Melissa in *The Hangover*, and macho Ted in *Bridesmaids*, who treats Annie like a piece of meat. They're nasty, flawed people who somehow threaten the protagonist's happiness, particularly if they're (obviously self-destructively) trying to connect emotionally with these unresolved characters. As an audience we're angry with the protagonist for putting themselves in this position, but we also know they deserve it. We are then able to delight in the vengeful payback when the protagonist wises up and gets even.

Secondly, diffusion appears when each of the characters is as narcissistic as each other – products of a selfish and greedy world. The Coen Brothers' *Intolerable Cruelty* goes for the metaphoric jugular in its even-handed attack on the ugly behaviour of a divorcing couple.

Thirdly, anger is diffused through the protagonist as perpetuator. If your protagonist takes pleasure in causing hurt to others, the audience might gain some delight from their pathological problem. Shallow Hal in *Shallow Hal*, who judges women on beauty alone, has to be hypnotised to see inner beauty. We can laugh at his shallow self, not only because it's a monumental blind spot, but because he'll ultimately hurt himself and end up alone. As the spell bursts, Hal reverts back to his own shallow self, deeply hurting the overweight Rosemary. It takes a huge dollop of humanity-inducing medicine for him to finally appreciate the destructiveness of his own superficiality.

In the romantic comedy, cruel protagonists who 'get better' are those who work on their issues, leading them to finally get the girl/guy, become healthier and happier, and generally 'win the day'. Female protagonists who have 'issues' can learn their lessons and win the guy too, just like manipulative and control-freak boss Margaret in *The Proposal*. However, Mavis in *Young Adult* and Julianne in *My Best Friend's Wedding* both learn that getting the guy is actually not what they need – self-love is. In *Identity Thief*, criminal Diana comes to terms with how her behaviour of ripping people off is actually ripping herself off from a chance of happiness and valuing people. She pays the price with prison but gains a close family who care for her.

THE TONE OF AWKWARDNESS

Awkwardness is the kind of emotional tone that is generated by comedy that plays on the audience's anxiety about relationships and repression of desires – as opposed to anger, which capitalises on more clear-cut dynamics. It makes audiences feel uncomfortable because we identify with the fact that relationships are not black and white, but are in fact made up of a zillion shades of grey – and it's really hard to be open and vulnerable to others.

Awkwardness is ultimately a tone that makes fun of the mask of self-protection. The dynamics of embarrassment, unpredictability, avoidance, detachment, alienation, aloofness, commitment-phobia and inexplicable reactions all serve the tonal emotion of awkwardness. It can be seen in many romantic comedies, and can be extreme and shocking as well as subtly contradictory. The classic moment in *When Sally Met Harry* when Sally fakes an orgasm in the café is an unforgettable moment of awkwardness that causes great mirth, partly due to extreme irreverence. At the indie end of the spectrum, the awkward tone can also be quirky. The highly understated interactions between characters in many Wes Anderson films, where quite emotional and open expressions are spoken in an almost flat way, is strange yet endearing to watch. There's an awkwardness to the stylised monotone, particularly when it's suddenly broken by physical comedy or more highly charged emotions like crying. In quirky action/sorocom *Violet and Daisy*, the deadpan expressions and 'cute' understated exchanges of the teenage assassins are suddenly interrupted by us finding out that Violet was raped, and we see her crying alone after meeting her oppressors.

As a writer, you'll enjoy creating awkwardness in a romantic comedy if you're fascinated by complexity and ambiguity in human relationships, and if you're more interested in what people don't or can't say than what they do or can. You probably take pleasure from the gulf and gaps between people – the longing that they generate as well as the open-ended nature of awkward dynamics. You may be mistrustful of people's agenda. You might have a more anxious disposition about being exposed and made vulnerable yourself in relationships. You might want to create characters who are awkward, alone, uncomfortable and inadequate, and through them show the world that it's hard being human. You're probably comfortable with flux and evolution rather than closure and happy resolutions. Quirkiness, matter-of-fact utterances, deadpan expressions, detachment, sarcasm, irony, neurosis, bizarre happenings, subversion, avoidance and repression can all be comic examples of the tone of awkwardness. Subtextual dialogue, voice-over, monologue and surrealism are all useful devices for establishing awkwardness.

The audience has a more testing experience watching a film where the awkward tone dominates, because they have to keep guessing – predictability is not emphasised. Unsurprisingly, the awkward tone is alive and kicking in many independent romantic comedies. The protagonists of Woody Allen, Julie Delpy and Nicole Holofcener are effective at generating this tone as a major form of comedy in their romantic comedies/dramedies. Charlie Kaufman's *Eternal Sunshine of the Spotless Mind* and *Adaptation* feature protagonists and love relationships that are elusive, contrary and layered with meaning. Mainstream romcoms can also have their awkward moments. The awkward tone can appear in mainstream feel-good movies such as *Couples Retreat*. Here, the perfectionist control-freak couple, Jason and Cynthia, present their relationship therapist with a detailed document about their history as a couple – their strengths and weaknesses – as if they were in fact a failed business enterprise rather than a couple with emotional needs and painful situations they can't control.

THE TONE OF COMPASSION

Compassion is the tonal emotion that will literally pull at your heartstrings when writing. You want the audience to really feel for, if not wallow in, the romantic emotional plight of your protagonists – to share their pain, to commit to following the twists and turns of their emotional love journey, and to celebrate their successes in finding happiness. In other words, a compassionate tone is all about empathy and commitment to the character. It's about seeing people in a gentle way, being non-critical and caring about them, and being motivated by acceptance, understanding and hope. Feeling compassion, for writers, means you really know and understand your characters inside and out, 'warts 'n' all'. With a compassionate tone, we generally smile with the character as they learn lessons about love, and are deeply concerned for the outcome rather than laughing at them or finding them ridiculous. As is probably obvious, compassion is arguably the most frequently used emotional tone in writing romantic comedies.

As a writer seeking to generate the emotional tone of compassion, you might believe that 'emotional truth' is driving you, and that audiences derive most of their pleasure from identifying with emotionally satisfying and generally uplifting stories.

Compassionate-feeling films don't tend to have many angry tonal moments in them. Compassion is not about retaliation, vengeance, or a need to win. You won't be creating characters who are inherently bad, so much so that they can never change. In *The Best Exotic Marigold Hotel*, for example, Jean is depicted as a woman who has fallen out of love with her husband, needs to be near her daughter and is relieved her old age isn't going to be so poverty-stricken after all. With a few harsher tones, her characterisation could tip nearer that of a stereotypically nagging wife only out for herself, but we're given enough story information to understand her plight and see her reaction as a coping mechanism.

THE TONE OF IDEALISM

The ultimate feel-good factor of a romantic comedy is generated by the tone of idealism, one that pulls no punches when it comes to shameless sentimentality and uber-positivity – what romantic comedies are best known for. The emotional tone of idealism is also why so many romantic comedies have a bad reputation – for being too sugary, too gushing and too like fairy tales. Those critical of romcoms that show too many perfect worlds, beautiful people and lives that are only unfulfilled because of a failure in love, or where failure in love is seen as the ultimate failure, are simply antagonised by this tone. It's unashamedly an escapist tone that can often dominate Act Three of a classic romcom, after the crisis, in which happy resolutions dominate and joy and happiness are pretty much unadulterated. The tone can be seen as a form of denial – a refusal to let too much darkness, reality or emotional truth creep in and ruin the dream. But that can be one of the successful elements of the genre, too, and why super-positive romcoms that are marketed effectively pull in big audiences.

The tone of idealism on the whole supports the belief that there's someone out there for everybody – that no matter how lonely, misguided or unresolved the main character is, or how dark times are, the perfect match exists. The idealistic tone rarely comes along in a film with a main character who's perfectly happy playing the field in lifelong non-monogamy, but Samantha in *Sex and the City 2* is a good example of a highly attractive, successful and sexually free woman who doesn't want children, doesn't want a soulmate and gets enough emotional support from her friends.

Just like its opposite, the angry tone, stereotypes can serve the idealistic tone, particularly with secondary and tertiary characters. But unlike the angry tone, in which the stereotypical character doesn't really change, the idealistic tone can subvert them. *Mamma Mia!* shows a large Greek peasant woman trudging along next to her husband, carrying sticks on her back as he rides the donkey. She hears the music, throws the sticks away, and joins the female Bacchanalian revels to the song *Dancing Queen* – and looks truly jubilant and free.

The idealistic tone can be 'warmly funny' due to the fact it's most often delivered in a way that puts a smile on our faces. Sheer joy, extreme exuberance and overwhelming openness in terms of emotional expressiveness are all hallmarks of scenes where idealism is at play. Is it a tone preferred by women? Do more men cringe at a feel-good, emotionally expressive vibe, conflicting with what can still be expected from male behaviour? As a writer you might want your characters singing, dancing and full of joy, if only metaphorically. Bollywood is a good example of an industry that produces films where the emotional tone of idealism is pervasive. In these films, characters come together in a show of unity and togetherness through song and dance, creating warmth in the audience.

While our gender-defined lives certainly do shape our experiences of and hopes for romance and relationships, the idealistic tone can be seen in films that have both male and female protagonists. Super-idealistic romantic comedies emphasise heterosexual monogamy as the ultimate fulfilling achievement for our emotional and family lives, which of course may annoy you as a writer, and may impel you to tell a different story.

The pleasantness of make-believe is one of the joys of childhood and innocent, imaginative play. Perhaps the idealistic tone in romantic comedy is our adult way of reminding ourselves of the sheer hope, delight and security of being unconditionally loved and protected – something our stressed-out adult worlds don't easily permit. If we get off on the brutality of action, crime and horror, the pleasure of the romcom, despite all its cheesiness, gets many more brownie points for spreading peace and love!

SAD AND TRAGIC TONES

Most romantic comedies contain different emotional tones, which is part of their success at striking the feel-good vibe that audiences crave. Writers can mix them up to entertain, delight, amuse, and elicit empathy from their audience in equal measures. It's fair to say that the emotional spectrum of tone in romantic comedy tends to limit the darker tones that come along with drama, thriller and dramatic romances. Situations in which the character faces death, pain and loss, and devastating situations that love and the support of others cannot remedy, are few and far between in the romcom genre. Where there is loss, such as death of a loved one, it's depicted gently and with great tenderness, bringing characters together. Where a character is at the 'end of their rope', a spark of optimism will usually shift their perspective, or a friend will turn up in their hour of need. Sometimes, a tragi-comic feel is achieved by the writer skilfully weaving blatant irony into a situation, which 'tones up' the darkness – or at least gives the audience a chance for a wry smile.

This solution-focused handling of what are in essence dramatic moments can ensure that an overall tonal consistency is maintained in your screenplay. If creating a story is like weaving a tapestry, then tones are taken from feel-good skeins with many different coloured strands and slubs.

Just because jarring and shocking dark or bleak events tend to be avoided, it doesn't mean you can't work them in. If something unexpected appeals to you, the best advice is to try it. Genres change and grow because of risk-taking by the writer and filmmaking team. Besides, it can always be changed in development if feedback suggests the tone is too inconsistent.

CASE STUDY: *ABOUT TIME*

About Time is a young man's 'fantasy bromantic famcom' in which a special inherited gift passed down through a family's male line brings a father and son closer.

It tells the story of Tim, a young man who has had an idyllic childhood growing up in Cornwall, and his love for his family and future wife. In fact, idyllic permeates as the dominant tone through the whole narrative. Tim inhabits a wonderful life of privilege in both Cornwall and London, where people are able to pursue their career dreams, live in a wealthy and cultured world, and generally exude 'success'. The beautiful life symbolism surrounds us in the film's feel-good escapist tone, supported by Tim's bouncy and witty voice-over.

Somewhat originally for a romantic comedy, *About Time* contains a fantasy element of time travel. The male members of the family have a special gift – the ability to travel back in time and alter the course of events and situations. It isn't explained why only the males have this gift, but the theme of male friendship and father-son 'lessons' to each other permeates the stronger of the film's two close relationships. The perfect world of privilege is counterbalanced by a strongly spiritual and existential layer of themes, created by the fantasy device of time travel in which Tim can alter his fate and those of the people he loves to make things – emotional problems and matters of the heart – better.

Tim uses time travel to put things right in his love life, creating comedy through irony and out-doing the normal course of fate. First, he tries to get into bed with super-hot friend-of-the-family Charlotte, a blonde 'goddess'. Despite his efforts and the magical chance to redo certain situations, she always manages to shift the goalposts to avoid getting intimate with him. Tim learns he can't make anyone love him if they just don't. Later, he uses his gift again to find Mary, 'the one', after a chance encounter at a dining-in-the-dark restaurant. Unfortunately, Tim's need to be a nice guy conflicts with his love life when he has to go back in time to help the playwright who's putting him up – he can't help him and have the date. And so he loses Mary.

He remembers her love of Kate Moss, the subject of a Testino exhibition, and so manages to contrive a second 'meet cute' – only to learn that this time she's already acquired a boyfriend. Tim has to painfully extract details of the date, time and place they met so he can go back in time to prevent Mary and her new boyfriend from meeting. He can also use the time-travelling gift to make sure he improves on his sexual performance on their first date, another funny moment. Dating, co-habiting, marriage and their first baby follows, Tim not needing his gift again until his sister Kit Kat's depression leads to her drunk driving and crashing the car. By going back in time, to prevent her from meeting the selfish boyfriend who contributed to her low-self-esteem, Tim thinks he's sorted out his problem – only to find out that his baby girl has changed to being a boy!

Consulting his father, Tim learns that if he goes back and alters life before conception the baby will not necessarily be the same one. It's here that Tim is confronted with a horrible choice – he truly loves his first baby girl and can't bear the thought of replacing her with someone he hasn't bonded with, let alone remember conceiving. Tim realises what he can offer Kit Kat instead is unconditional support by being there for her, helping her through the dark times, and helping her find a better boyfriend.

Finally, Tim's gift is used to spend quality time with Dad in his final months before dying of cancer. When he goes back in time during the funeral to spend some moments with him, father gives son some words of advice for using their magical gift properly – literally reliving each day as it comes and appreciating people, giving back and doing what he can to make people feel better. Eventually, Tim gives up time travel when he realises he doesn't need it anymore – he's learnt to live fully 'in the now' with happiness, appreciation and an open heart.

The tone of idealism is achieved by avoiding unpleasantness or emotional ugliness in how the characters relate to each other. Father and son are emotionally warm and positively expressive to each other – even more so than Tim and Mary – in a heartfelt way. A residual 'angry' tone is very subtly woven in to break the idealism, but only through secondary characters. Mary explodes one night while Tim remains a saint throughout. Brittleness comes with the stiff-upper-lip of Mum, who is super British in an unemotionally quirky way. Mary's parents are conventionally repressed Republicans who don't even attend the wedding. A sexually stereotypical comedic tone is achieved through the character of Joanna, who is chiefly characterised as sex-obsessed. A darker and more irreverent tone is delivered through the raging of verbally abusive playwright Rory, who lives alone, is divorced, hates babies, and calls his daughter a slut; this injects a subtly comedic misogynistic and misanthropic element into the tone.

Being essentially a nice guy without any obvious emotional flaws or struggles of his own, in a world where life's struggles are emotional and only seemingly suffered by other characters such as Kit Kat, Tim's journey in *About Time* isn't the typically overt transformational change/character arc familiar from many romantic comedies. It's ultimately a gentle story of Tim's rite of passage through a series of gentle and humanistic lessons, to being a fully engaged, appreciative, present and loving husband and father. We might say that it's about a nice and positive guy learning to become even nicer and more positive – so it's super-feel-good because we don't have to worry about Tim not healing his negative traits, as he doesn't actually possess any. Like father, like son. In this way, *About Time* manages to blend the tones of idealism with an element of compassion woven throughout the narrative, with the occasional splash of anger – creating a truly escapist bubble with a gentle philosophical core.

HOT TIPS

- Romcoms can age because the ranges of tone can go in and out of fashion.

- Dramedic tone is currently in the zeitgeist. Farce doesn't dominate romcoms on the whole, but is used selectively.

- Characters can have many tones. The more minor the character, the more 'one note' the tone. The protagonist can be drawn with many comedic tones, or can remain fairly simple in tone, but has to engage with secondary characters drawn with differing tones.

- Select your favourite tones for your own romcom and think about the ones you've avoided. Force yourself to imagine scenes or situations where these tones can be used for comic effect.

WHO LOVES YOU, BABY?

You probably know the expression *character is story*. Well, in a romantic comedy character is *love story*. It's your job as a screenwriter to create a character who's so unique that they can only lead a unique love story – one we've never seen because we've never met your character before. Ideally, not even somebody similar. Now it's time to focus on the first step of discovering and creating your romantic comedy protagonist. The eventual story this character compels you to take them on will be explored in Chapter 6 – Love Lessons. For now, we'll introduce some of the key factors that you can work with to create a truly fabulous protagonist. They're not prescriptive but, as always, aim to support your ideas as they develop, with the ultimate aim of strengthening your romcom and making it more saleable.

By undertaking an intensive process of character development, you'll be in a better position to know answers – hopefully more original ones – to the following questions:

- Why is this character the best one for the kind of romcom story I want to tell?

- Why is this character worth travelling the distance with – for me and my audience?

- What's unique and memorable about them? How is this so?

- What are the character's issues/problems/factors affecting their ability to 'love' – themselves and other people – or to connect with others in a satisfying and healthy way?

- If they don't have issues, what's their real function in the story?

- Why is my character attracted to the other person/persons? Why do they have strong feelings for them?

- How does my character feel about intimacy?

- What does romantic love mean to my character?

- How does my character represent my own thoughts about love – and do they help me to tell the kind of story I envision and want to write?

- When it comes down to it, is my main character really a version of me? Are their issues my issues? If so, what am I telling myself about love and/or connecting with others?

It might be quite useful to ask yourself these questions now, and jot down the answers. You can review them in later drafts as your understanding and intentions for your main characters develop.

If you take romantic comedy as the all-encompassing super-genre, it's virtually impossible to define any unifying trait in their protagonists other than *they have strong feelings for another human being*. Those feelings can be passionate, angry, hateful, joyful, obsessive, lustful, deranging, confused, hurt, delightful, fascinated, helpful, unhelpful or downright destructive – but always with a sense of humour (depending on your tonal preferences). The point is, they're overwhelming to your character and will form the main engine of the screenplay. It's those strong feelings that'll take centre stage as your character travels a primarily emotional journey, dealing with the other person(s) and resolving – or not – their strong feelings for them. And it'll be the nature of that journey that's shaped by those feelings.

GOING THE DISTANCE WITH YOUR CHARACTER

Depending on whether you start with something high-concept – 'It's about a werewolf who falls in love with a stripper' – or a specific character portrait – 'It's about the young Queen Victoria falling in love with a young Albert' – your biggest challenge will be creating that character and making them memorable, unique and sufficiently entertaining that an audience is happy to go the distance with them. Learning who that individual character really is, not to mention the person or 'thing' she/he/it has feelings for, will be probably be the most time-consuming and challenging aspect to the entire process of developing your screenplay. It's just like falling in love/lust at first sight, when the person you see at the start and make all kinds of assumptions about based on their looks certainly isn't who they really are inside – or, more to the point, who they'll be after years of togetherness.

With your romantic comedy protagonist, who you start out with at the beginning isn't necessarily who you'll end up with. Characters can undergo such huge transformations in development that their name, age, sex, race and personality traits might change radically. But the long haul in character development, like a good marriage, is worth it. Taking feedback, self-examination, knowing when to compromise – all of which are essential to a functioning relationship that can go the distance – will bring great results with your character. You'll get to the point when your characters live and breathe – when they take on lives of their own and you know the external masks they hide behind, all their defence mechanisms and all of their good, bad and ugly sides. In this way, they drive the love story because they're fully fleshed out, complex, relatable individuals with minds – and story desires – of their own.

....

EXERCISE – WHAT'S THEIR STORY?

The purpose of this exercise is to develop your observational skills about people, and to study actions and behaviour as a means of communication.

Go to a bar, a restaurant, a museum, a tourist attraction, a market – or somewhere like that – and do some serious people-watching. Ideally choose a place where you can see couples in action. Try to avoid a train, which tends to zombiefy people on long journeys! The idea is for you to do some 'couple watching' so you're inspired to draw creative conclusions from what you see and sense.

- Make up a story about who they are, based on what they're wearing, how they carry themselves and their general vibe.

- Give the couple pretend names.

- Study the interactions between the couple and imagine: how long have they been together? What's the state of their relationship now? How do they feel about each other? What's their future?

- Now write a scene about what happens when they get home from this place. How do they act with each other? How might their visit to this place affect what happens when they get home?

....

CHARACTER DEMOGRAPHICS

Choosing the protagonist/s of your romantic comedy is on the surface the easiest thing to do in screenwriting. No character, no story, remember? You probably know they're male, female, transsexual or gender neutral, their broad age, the colour of their skin, their culture, marital status, their job, their economic status, where they live – and you might even know their name. You might also know some quirky and specific things about them, like they have blue hair or a pet fish called Wanda... but we'll get to that later.

In other words, you're probably typecasting your character from the outset, even subconsciously. We can't help but categorise people according to the ways our culture defines people – and we instinctively know a certain person with certain characteristics is the one we want to lead the story.

Who you choose to be your protagonist says quite a lot about you; in fact – you'll have singled out a 'type' to make certain statements in your story about people like this, and what love means to them. An initial demographic approach can be useful in enabling you to explore some of the attitudes and values you have about 'types' of people – and this can have an insidious effect on the themes and messages, intended or otherwise, your story sends out to an audience.

By 'typecasting' we broadly mean the demographics that your cast of characters – if you think of them like a population in their own little universe – reflect. Does this sound a bit odd? Aren't we supposed to be helping you create unique and individual characters? Well, the good news is that a bit of typecasting of your one or two protagonists early on in development is actually very useful in helping you achieve uniqueness – not only through your characters, but also in your screenplay's message as conveyed by the experience of those 'types' of characters.

By character demographics we mean:

- Name and address
- Age
- Sex
- Ethnic group
- Ability
- Religion
- Economic status
- Employment status
- Nature of employment
- Marital status
- Health status
- Other people in the household
- Level of education

In fact, all the kinds of things that are written in a real-world census.

For example, in *The 40-Year-Old Virgin* protagonist Andy is a white, early-middle-aged, middle-class, able-bodied, heterosexual man. He works in an electronics store, lives alone and is unmarried. He has disposable income, enough to enable him to build a huge collection of superhero model toys. From the demographics of Western society, Andy is representative of the supposedly most powerful

WRITING AND SELLING ROMANTIC COMEDY SCREENPLAYS

social group – the white, middle-aged male, the 'average Joe'. But in the film he's the weakest and most vulnerable, so there's some obvious subversion going on here. For audiences used to the status attached to wider Western demographics, Andy is exactly the right 'type' to use to show how hard it is to be a loser guy when you're supposed to be – type-wise – at the top of the food chain.

Demographics also help you to decide when stereotyping is useful for your romcom (as it very often is), or when it results in just bad characterisation. In *The 40-Year-Old Virgin*, nymphomaniac Beth is stereotypical as the sexually ravenous dysfunctional man-eater. She's single, young, blonde and attractive – the 'type' that most men are supposed to sexually desire, when in fact she's a living nightmare. Beth also serves what could be said is an underlying theme of the film: that, if anything, 'alpha' characteristics in males and females are more harmful than helpful.

So who turns out to be right for Andy, other than his bromantic fraternity of guys who work at the electronics store? It's Trish, a white, middle-class single mother of a daughter, who runs an eBay shop reflecting her financial insecurity. As Andy's main goal is to lose his virginity, his emotional need is to be able to let someone in. Trish is non-threatening in terms of demographics, whereas Beth is.

While basic demographics can seem essentialist and obvious, you can treat them as the first stage in the incredibly in-depth process that creating a romantic comedy protagonist will involve. They can also help you to think about your audience and the saleability of your film. For example, while a trans story might be highly original and become critically acclaimed, would it help you to reach big box-office success, if that's important to you? If we look at *Mamma Mia!*, that was a huge success with cross-generational groups of females – but what did that do to challenge social demographics and gender representations?

Regardless, working with the basic demographics of your story world can be useful in character development, particularly if you're a writer who likes to categorise first and flesh out later. (This might also mean you're someone who likes to work out plot and structure before character – nothing wrong with that, we all do things differently.) If you're initially character-driven in approach, labelling and categories will probably repel you on some level, but they can still be useful for forcing yourself to think more widely about the place in the world your character takes.

....

EXERCISE - INDULGE YOURSELF IN TYPECASTING

This is an exercise to help you typecast your film's population. You can do this exercise if you know your characters (i.e. they already exist in your imagination or on the page) or even if you're at a very early stage in the development process – but try to do it early on.

Start with your main characters – the two who are 'overwhelmed' by each other and provide the central relationship of the romcom.

Imagine one of your main protagonists opening the door to a census interviewer. How would they label themselves, according to the demographic categories listed above?

Try not to think too hard about your answers at this point – just go with what feels right for your character.

Now go through the same process with your other main character – the 'object' of your first main character's affections/repulsions. You might find as you go through the exercise that you will be seeking to make them as different as possible. It might be that they come from a very similar community, or even type of family.

Then go through the process with the main secondary and tertiary characters.

Finally, reflect on the whole cast/population of your screenplay. What values are you attaching to demographic types in this world? Who is high status? Who is low, and why? What demographics suggest vulnerability? How does this compare with the status and values attached to your own culture's demographics?

Finished? Hopefully you've ended up with two character blueprints, if not the whole cast. But you should also be burning with the desire to make these people alive and kicking as individuals!

....

THE RELATIONSHIP ORIENTATION PARADIGM

Romantic comedy protagonists can fall into one or more of the following 'relationship orientation' categories. Depending on the structure and themes of your screenplay, characters can fall within one, two or several of these types. Your task is to make the character's problem unique to them. The categories can help you begin to focus on the nature of the character's main problem, understand why they have it in the first place, and decide whether or not you want them to get over it.

THE BORN LONER

Introverted types, according to Jung, derive an awful lot of satisfaction from their own company, unlike extroverts who need 'the other' to share and bounce off. We're all a little bit of both but the Born Loner is a character type who, deep down, doesn't need anyone else for emotional fulfilment. They're good at having hobbies, ambitions and passions that don't involve close interaction with another person. It's not that they don't like or need the company of others; they just have a fundamental allegiance to themselves. Sharing can be hard for them because they don't really see the need.

Born Loners can often be married and have children, however. Two Born Loners could live a very harmonious life together, respectful of each other's space. A Born Loner and their opposite, the Eternally Devoted, might have more passion, however – never feeling the other one quite 'gets' them. Born Loners can seem secretive because they don't feel the need to offload, but in fact verbal 'sharing' makes them feel threatened. Born Loners can be deeply spiritual types who only need a god for company. Born Loners in romcoms are Megan in *Bridesmaids*, Mavis in *Young Adult*, Ashburn and Mullins in *The Heat*, and Arnold in *Hope Springs*.

THE SCARED OF BEING ALONE

The Scared of Being Alone type doesn't like to be single. They can be loyal and adoring partners, or serial monogamists, but don't be under any illusion that this character won't move on fast when the romance fades. Scared of Being Alone types do not like their own company, for reasons you may wish to work out in your character. Jack in bromedy *Sideways* is a good example of the unfaithful boychild who always needs a woman, despite his commitments. *Runaway Bride* gives another love 'em and leave 'em type. Pragmatism and keeping all options open are central values to this character. They can be nomadic people, too, who gather no moss, constantly rolling from one relationship – or bed – to another.

THE STUCK ALONE

The Stuck Alone character is unable to find love – or, in the case of dramedy, self-respect – because they have an unresolved emotional difficulty or difficulties. In other words, this type reflects the human condition, not just the vast majority of romcom protagonists. The character is 'stuck' because they keep coming up against the same old problems. They haven't grown emotionally, and your job as writer is to put them on a journey where they have to confront the issues that keep them separate from others. In *Enough Said*, Eva is a divorcee who hasn't gained closure on the breakdown of her own marriage and dreads the second 'loss' of her daughter going off to university. To cope with these two unbearable situations, she has unconscious strategies of protecting herself. These involve denigrating and detaching from her new boyfriend, Albert, and replacing her daughter emotionally by getting close to her daughter's best friend.

THE UNLUCKY IN LOVE

This is the character who actively wants a relationship, and who doesn't have any real major issues but can't seem to keep or attract a mate for reasons beyond their control. They might be physically challenged, for instance, like Phillippe, a once-privileged aristocrat who becomes quadriplegic in bromance dramedy *The Intouchables*. Some Unlucky in Love characters might have married someone who falls in love with someone else. They might be socially excluded, the bottom of the heap, or not be rich in a world that only values wealth and power. The primary cause of distress for the Unlucky in Love is the fact that life isn't fair, that external factors prevent them from succeeding in love and they need to find the rare special other who can accept them for who they are. The Unlucky in Love character is painfully alone. Frances in *Frances Ha* describes herself as 'undateable'. She's larger than life, too much, too tall, too gauche and awkward. The joke hides a deeper sorrow about her loneliness. Frances in romantic dramedy *Under the Tuscan Sun* is callously dumped and divorced, for no obvious flaw other than for being a good wife. In *Baggage Claim*, Montana is Unlucky in Love as the oldest female in her family not to be married, and goes to extreme lengths to find 'the one'.

THE ETERNALLY DEVOTED

This character is someone who literally lives for, and is defined by, their relationship. They will give their all to their partner, and forever more. They're someone who understands the notion of compromise, sharing and 'working at it' because they prioritise their relationship above all else. Even if they're on the surface practical, inside they'll have a gooey romantic heart. Eternally devoted males in romcoms include Mark Darcy in *Bridget Jones*, Tim in *About Time* and Rod the baseball player in *Jerry Maguire*. Females include Jane in *Austenland* – for Darcy – Latika in *Slumdog Millionaire* and Frances in *Frances Ha*.

CREATING UNIQUENESS

The other end of the spectrum from basic demographics is exploring the uniqueness of your romantic comedy character – all those traits, habits, attitudes, values, ways of being, ways of communication, ways of experiencing the world and ways of relating that make them who they are. Above all, it's about why they're attracted to or compelled by the significant other in your story, be that a classic romcom, a bromcom or a sorocom.

And so it's now time to think about the DNA of your character's personality, and how you're going to make sure that no two sets of DNA are alike. Go back to your character blueprint and start to visualise the human being behind the type. It's time to find out who they really are. What kinds of problems do they have relating to themselves and to others, and why do they have these problems?

....

EXERCISE – WHAT PROTAGONISTS WANT

This exercise is designed to help you define your character and their 'romantic' problem in more depth.

Ask your character:

- What do you want out of life?
- When are you at your happiest?
- What's your worst fear?
- If one thing could make you feel a lot better about life, what would it be?
- What's your idea of a perfect day?
- What's the longest you've been in a relationship?
- Who or what is the love of your life? Why?
- Who are your closest friends and family members? Why?
- What problems are you having in relationships?

- How often do you have sex? With whom? Describe your sex life, and what you like to give and get.
- Are you emotionally fulfilled? If not, why not? If so, how?
- How would you like to be remembered?

....

GOING IN DEEP

Psychoanalysis can be inspiring in defining characters' unique aspects, in terms of how they relate to themselves and to others. Theories of personality are only that – attempts to explain the fusion of nature and nurture in producing an individual. As a writer, you can utilise any theory you wish in the creation of your character – all meaning is there to be plundered for art!

Because a romantic comedy is about a character who's essentially obsessed by another character (or characters, in the famcom for example), acting the shrink can be a useful position to take as a writer. It can help you to get inside all your characters' minds and really find out what makes them tick, alone and together. Of course there's a lot of creative guesswork to this approach – you don't have to be any kind of 'expert' to produce a convincing character, as characters don't emerge only from theories! They can emerge from your own unconscious, for a start!

ID, EGO AND SUPEREGO

Thanks to Freud, as a writer you can utilise his definitions of the unconscious to explore your character's dynamic relationships – with themselves and with others.

The *id* is all about instant and infantile gratification – the id wants and the id tries to get. Food, comfort, sex, death – see the id as your character's wildest fantasies and desires. What keeps the id in check? The *ego*. Not an ego as in a 'huge narcissistic pain in the neck', but a hardworking diplomat that represents your character's ability to respond appropriately to situations. The ego wants to protect itself from out of control impulses, but also the opposite, rigid control. This is where the *superego* comes in – the control freak trying to take over your character's mind with its moral agenda. Righteous, controlling, moralistic and judgemental, the superego is all about inflexible, constraining codes of conduct, and right and wrong.

If a character falls in love with their best friend's partner, the id would want him or her to declare the love, give up the friendship, have rampant sex and satisfy the craving. The superego would absolutely forbid such disloyal antics. The ego would be the middleman, acknowledging that the id has certain needs and fantasies are fun, but that to cave into them could lead to emotional chaos, breakdown and loss. The ego would also have to remind the disapproving superego that fantasy isn't harmful, and that if two people are right for each other, perhaps 'going for it' isn't such a bad thing. The ego would do a lot of weighing up before rushing into things.

The ego has to do so much hard work that it employs a range of 'defence mechanisms' – a mental box of tricks to manage the hassle of being human. If this sounds complicated enough in one person, obviously no film shows man or woman as an island, so knowing how your main character's mind works isn't enough. It's a good idea to take the same psychoanalytical approach to thinking about how one person's defences blend with another's. Emotional issues have to have a degree of compatibility at the end of the day.

In short, interpersonal dynamics get only more complex in the romantic comedy. Here are some of them, and how characters have manifested them.

PROJECTION

Rather than too much self-criticism, how much easier is it for the ego to blame someone else? We project when we don't want to admit our weaknesses, flaws, vices and bad patterns, and hey presto – we can easily single out somebody else to criticise for having the exact same problem! Projection means we can avoid self-examination because it's too painful. Projection can also come out of envy – when we feel resentful that somebody else is so lucky and gifted. In romcoms, projection is rife when the protagonist loathes and detests the 'object' of their affection/desire because they haven't yet come to terms with their own negative traits. Far easier to curse and yell at the loved one. It normally means they have some emotional growth to do to stop letting this trait damage their relationships, or they need to develop the very quality they envy. Arnold in *Hope Springs* projects resentment against the counsellor because he feels inadequate in terms of sexual knowledge and – key – he doesn't know his wife as well as the counsellor does.

DISPLACEMENT

This is nothing other than having a safe target. Displacement is an unconscious way of taking out frustrations on someone other than the cause of those frustrations. Think of all the times you've been upset deeply by someone you love or an impossible personal situation, only to find yourself shouting at a stranger or just being mean to somebody who hasn't done anything bad. Why? Because the originator of the pain is, for some reason, unassailable – for example, they might be ill, a boss, a child or a violent bully. Bill from *Muriel's Wedding* takes out his anger at himself and all that he hasn't achieved in life by verbally and psychologically attacking his wife and children. This is in part what propels Muriel to find love – to prove that she is someone.

DENIAL

For whatever reason, your character doesn't want to face painful or uncomfortable thoughts or realities, and so banishes them to the unconscious. This is a form of *repression*. Sometimes denial is sensible – such as a coping mechanism after trauma. But if the scars of the trauma are causing ongoing issues, then denial isn't working anymore – the thoughts that have been repressed are affecting the character. Modern psychology is built on the premise that facing up

WHO LOVES YOU, BABY?

to old wounds or current pain is a way of gaining closure, or making the unacceptable manageable. Many romantic comedies all have characters with unresolved issues, but to what extent they go into depth about these varies greatly, most often because 'bad stuff' has to fit the tone. In *This is 40*, Pete is in denial about the full extent of his economic woes, wanting to protect himself and his wife from the truth, but is really unable to face up to his own fear of failure.

Miles in dramedy bromance *Sideways* is in denial about the fact that he's not very good as a writer. To admit it will be one more failure and rejection on top of his father's suicide and his failed marriage. He's lying to himself to protect himself. But repression isn't working – he's depressed, lonely, lying to himself and everyone he knows, likening himself to delicate grape pinot noir without realising it, and even stealing from his mother like a naughty and angry child. When he meets Maya, she's clearly right for the potential Miles but not the 'in denial' Miles. He thus has to face his worst fears and survive them to emerge capable of healthy love.

IDEALISATION

Close to denial is idealisation. We all know the romantic hero or heroine who obsesses over someone totally inappropriate for them (remember Bridget Jones' inappropriate worship of all things Daniel Cleaver?) while the 'right' one stands in the wings waiting for their beloved to come to their senses. In *(500) Days of Summer*, Tom is almost masochistic in his obsessional feelings for the unreliable Summer. Idealisation is a defence mechanism to avoid the painful truth that things aren't perfect. It's really a way for the character to sell themselves into a situation by talking it up constantly, when it's blatantly obvious to everyone around them – and the audience – that it's a lie.

The need to idealise is another way of avoiding a sense of inadequacy. If we project ideal virtues and qualities onto another person we're connected to (through partnership), then we bask in their glory through the power of association. There's something a little bit masochistic about the idealiser – the Mother, Madonna, Whore complex is a pattern of behaviour in some men who compulsively sleep around, breaking hearts in mistress after mistress waiting for the long-promised divorce, yet seeing their wives as bastions of virtue.

REGRESSION

Growing up is hard to do, and we all want to retreat to the 'metaphoric womb' sometimes. This can take the form of id behaviour – childlike impulses, comfort food, sex addiction, thumb sucking, drugs and drink, self-mutilation and even suicide. Regressive communication includes sulking, rages, tantrums, spite and revenge. A character who's experiencing 'arrested development' and needs to grow up can spend most of the film in a regressive state, just like Elizabeth in *Bad Teacher*, who drinks, smokes and lies on the job.

In romcoms, regressive states often dominate the battle of the sexes. In *What Happens in Vegas*, a drunken one-night stand leads to a marriage that both Jack and Joy regret instantly the next day. When Jack wins a million dollars in a slot machine with a coin supplied by Joy, a war begins like two spoilt children fighting over a toy. Joy and Jack resent the parental authority of the divorce judge, who tells them to work at their marriage for six months. If either party fails to work at it, the judge will take the money. A series of repressed childlike antics comically unfolds with both Joy and Jack seriously out to sabotage each other to drive the other away. Nick, Dale and Kurt in retaliatory crime/bromedy *Horrible Bosses* decide to have their cruel bosses killed – an immature way of handling injustice, but something that the audience could probably relate to with some degree of pleasure.

RATIONALISATION AND INTELLECTUALISATION

These are both ways for the character to avoid unpleasant and 'messy' emotions. It's the Dr Spock syndrome for people who deeply fear chaos. Emotions and feelings are responses to human experience, good and bad. Culturally, we can be influenced by what's acceptable in our society in terms of expressing emotion – but families have their own cultures too, and how people were raised can influence characters deeply.

In men and women, there's a generalised belief that men are more rational, and women, due to fluctuating hormones and gender conditioning to be empathic, are far more emotional. Certainly there are enough closed-off men and women in romcoms doing the rounds – from Mark Darcy to Margaret in *The Proposal*, both of whom need an expressive and feeling other to help them discover feelings that need to be let out.

This is a very basic introduction to some principles, but hopefully enough to encourage some real dimension in your character development. If you want to read more about psychoanalytical theories, find the original writings of Freud, Jung, Benjamin, Klein, Murdock and many others. Their work is accessible and stimulating when relating it to your characters (or yourself!). You can also read William Indick's book *Psychology for Screenwriters*, which introduces key theories to help with character development.

....

EXERCISE – PLAYING COUPLES COUNSELLOR

Imagine your character meets a genius shrink at a bar. Choose one of the ego defence mechanisms listed above and an emotional situation that's directly caused it in your character. Write a scene of dialogue where your character offloads to this 'stranger' with this defence mechanism in play, not realising they're talking to a mind expert. Don't work too hard at it – quick work can be best – and definitely don't worry about playing doctor!

Next, write the same scene as if the character has gone to a shrink for help with their relationship difficulties. Psychoanalysts are trained to think in terms of the 'presenting problem' to assess what is the most dominant issue, from which deeper unresolved past problems might spring. Ask shrink-like questions that probe your character, and see if your character's answers are different now that they're in a professional setting.

Finally, take your couple to see a couples therapist together. (Watch *Hope Springs* if you really get stuck!) Get them to explain in turn their problems with each other. Then reflect on the defence mechanisms your characters might reveal.

The point of this exercise is to get to know your characters' emotional lives, dynamics and unconscious ways of dealing with themselves and others. On a deeply transformational journey, some of the ideas you generate here might be useful for thinking about original ways to 'set up' your character.

....

CHOOSING THE SIGNIFICANT OTHER

Where would Bridget be without Mark (*Bridget Jones' Diary*)? Miles without Jack (*Sideways*)? Or Vicky without Cristina (*Vicky Cristina Barcelona*)? Choose any of your own favourite romantic comedies, romantic dramedies, bromcoms and sorocoms to explore and understand what is just so appealing about the central relationship, enough to make us hold our attention through an entire 90 minutes. There are usually a number of factors that keep us watching in a successful romantic comedy:

- **The chemistry** – the unique blend of these two personalities coming up against each other or gelling together like glue?

- **The internal obstacles** – the work your characters have to do on themselves before they are 'fit' to be with, e.g. selfishness, meanness, hurt from a previous relationship, low self-esteem.

- **Values** – the complementary or opposite values they may share

- **The external obstacles** – family, friends, work or even controlling ideologies that get in the way of the couple.

It's never just one of these factors in a film, it's usually a combination of all of these.

Creating the central relationship is a huge amount of fun for the writer. Not just because you are getting to play 'god' with not one human destiny but two! Most writers tend to identify slightly more (even if it is just a tiny bit) with one of their protagonists in a romantic comedy, try as hard as they might to be even handed. Let's call this character the true 'protagonist' for whom you've done all that previous character development work. Now you've got to choose the right significant other in the central relationship. This will take just as much work, and in shaping this character you will inevitably go back to your protagonist and revisit some of the choices you have made.

In 'real life' our choice of partner or best friend (or lack of) at any given time, or however fleeting – says just as much about our relationship with ourselves as it does say about our relationship with the other. If our self-esteem is rock bottom and we might attract a string of relationships with people who somehow reinforce our self-perception until we want to change. Likewise, if we have too much self-regard, we will seek out people who reinforce our egos. These are simplistic generalisations, of course, because there are many covert and complex factors about power dynamics in relationships that remain hidden and that are constantly in flux over the course of a relationship. Your choice, as writer, of significant other in your romantic comedy will probably reflect on the state your protagonist is in, their sense of self-regard, and to what extent and how you want them to change.

How complicated or subtly nuanced or simplistic you want your central relationship to be will depend on the type of film you are making and the intended audience. Classic Hollywood romcoms tend to have pretty obvious opposite traits that the couple can learn from, whilst independent films can be far more layered. In *Ruby Sparks*, Calvin is remote, self-controlled and a little misanthropic, suffering from the failure of a previous relationship. He creates a fictional character Ruby who miraculously comes to life. He believes she is his perfect woman, and at first she is – autonomous, quirky, and lively. They have fun, fascinate each other and he is over the moon with his newfound soulmate. Of course, because he hasn't really had to face himself or change at all, his old patterns soon start getting the better of him. He becomes threatened by her autonomy and freedom – and worse, the fact she is acutally feeling entrapped by him. The old fear of rejection creeps in and soon begins to consume him. His answer, to 'rewrite her' to suit his low self-esteem. Gradually, he becomes a more extreme version of his previous self – a tyrannical bully. He literally shocks himself into becoming a better person, and letting her go. Ruby has no power at all; she is after all a product of his imagination, controlled and defined by her creator. She has no real agency in changing him. It is only his ugliness that does that, and that he destroyed the fleeing happiness he shared with Ruby when she was at her most autonomous. Hope comes at the end in the fact that he managed to reject his own tyranny for the risk of finding happiness with a real person, who he can't control.

EXERCISE – MATCHMAKING

In choosing your significant other (as in life!) you can ask yourself the following questions:

- If you met the significant other in a bar, how would you describe your friend the protagonist to them (particularly if you wanted to set them up)?
- Why would the significant other run a mile when first meeting the protagonist?
- Why would they hang around?
- What chemistry do they create together?
- How does the significant other threaten the protagonist?
- How does the significant other complement the protagonist's good points?
- What does the significant other stand to lose or gain by getting involved with the protagonist?

- What can the significant other teach the protagonist?
- What can the significant other learn from the protagonist?

....

EMOTIONAL TRUTH AND CHARACTER ARC

How does your character express themself emotionally? Do they have insight into themselves and others? A healthy ego normally means the character is able to be emotionally open with themselves and others – although this might be culturally specific. Very often, mainstream romantic comedies require the protagonist to do some serious soul-searching on their journey – to get to a point of emotional honesty with themselves by facing up to pain – before they're capable of a healthy, loving relationship.

Many independent romcoms – even where the filmmaker doesn't label them as such, because of the negative connotations that come with mainstream versions – do, however, show relatively emotionally articulate characters who probe themselves and others constantly. Woody Allen, Noah Baumbach and Julie Delpy all use articulate characters who go into emotional battles with their own neuroses and their objects of affection from the start. We see id, ego and superego all at work, revealing the complexity and rather unresolved nature of their connection with each other. This is quite different to the classic transformational journey, which tends to upfront id and superego conflicts that are limiting the character's possibility for healthy relationships at the start. The classic transformational arc thus represents the struggle of the ego to become healthier.

CHARACTER, GENDER AND THEME

Just as you're assigned a gender at birth, you'll do the same for your characters. Your character's identity will be monumentally affected by their attitude to their own gender, and to the gender expectations that surround them. For a whole host of exercises in working out your character's relationship with and 'negotiation' of their gender, you can read *The Woman in the Story: Creating Memorable Female Characters* by Helen Jacey. Most of the character exercises on feminine gender are apparently very useful if you apply them to men too!

By discovering and questioning your own unconscious attitudes about gender, you can decide what you want your own characters to represent. Do you believe most women really want to find a man to marry, have babies and be financially supported? Do you believe men find commitment harder? Do you believe in soulmates and happy-ever-after? Go back to your own attitudes and values about love, romance and commitment from earlier exercises and put them into practice. Perhaps you want to suggest that, actually, life is about loving many people and not necessarily one at a time, and that monogamy isn't easy?

If all that your female character wants (deep down) is true love, but her emotional problems are getting in the way, and your male character's obviously the perfect guy who comes to her emotional rescue, which she eventually appreciates after doing some work on herself, you're in mainstream and conventional romantic comedy and dramedic genre territory. *The Proposal* and *Sweet Home Alabama* both show successful career women learning that marriage to a good man is more fulfilling than work, and that finding a family is more rewarding. It's true that there aren't yet many romantic comedies about men realising their successful career is getting in the way of them finding true marital bliss, so there's some obvious sexual stereotyping going on. This more supports the family values lobby, which advocates that women should stay at home and be the primary carers of children.

On the other hand, while these kinds of romcoms annoy women who love their careers and don't see marriage as an either-or, such films aren't necessarily evil propaganda for those women in the audience who buy into this choice – of which there are many, including feminists! The same goes for 'queer theorists', who can live with the contradiction of being monogamous themselves while criticising films that espouse commitment in both men and women.

The romcom is definitely opening up to new explorations of romance, and while it's true there are still more happy endings that bring the characters together forever, this is no longer a requirement of the romcom. *(500) Days of Summer*, *The Break-Up*, *Ted* and *My Best Friend's Wedding* all show alternatives. There isn't a right or a wrong, but as a writer you can use characters to explore choices about love and how society expects us to conform or not. If you want to write a classic romcom – gay or straight – just because you put a wedding in the story, it doesn't mean that it's a bad film!

QUICK **INSIGHT**

Jeff Reno, screenwriter, talking about romantic comedy with David Misch, screenwriter and author of Funny: The Book/Everything You Always Wanted To Know About Comedy.

JR: Most romantic comedy has some kind of obstacle keeping the two people apart. It's very specific to the genre that two people want to be together, but have something stopping them. Earlier, say the romantic comedy of the 30s and 40s, one of the most common obstacles was class differences, different stations in life for the couple. That waned over the years.

DM: You'd still have characteristic differences. She's uptight, he's laid-back.

JR: It was interesting in *Notting Hill* that there was the class difference, bookstore worker and movie star, and in *Pretty Woman*, a prostitute and a millionaire. They seemed to be hearkening back to the old ones. The thing that almost always separates the good ones from the bad ones is intelligence. Smart, funny dialogue and a certain level of intelligence in the execution. People talk about chemistry all the time but I've always been of the mind that a large percentage of chemistry comes down to the words they are saying and the story underneath. That's a writer's bias obviously. It's obviously a huge advantage having good actors deliver the dialogue with the kind of charm that makes you care about them and the relationship. But the wit is usually what made the great ones work. Nowadays too many are just mildly amusing. Lately it's all a bit 'real' where it used to be very stylised dialogue, slightly heightened, which to my mind made it a little more entertaining. I miss that a lot.

DM: Romcom is the only genre where, from the beginning, women have been allowed to be as intelligent, strong and equal, essentially, as men. And that has been to its benefit. Women have not attained that status in pretty much any other genre.

Why do stupid things work? Look at *The Hangover*. The boys are driving those movies. With *Bridesmaids* you have slapstick but you've got great, clearly drawn characters and a great story.

JR: *Annie Hall* is one I've always aspired to. Woody Allen was subverting the genre while doing it. *Annie Hall* wasn't linear, it went backward and forward, to his childhood even, and the biggest subversion of all was an ending where they don't end up together. But you still felt satisfied. It was still a great film – it won an Oscar. It had a very thoughtful ending. It was about love, but that didn't mean these two had to be together. And the audience turned up. You do it in a smart enough way, they will go.

DM: Everything you said could be applied to *(500) Days of Summer*. They told the story in an unusual way, they did not stay together, and the audience went out feeling great.

JR: It's really interesting with *(500) Days of Summer*, same thing, deconstructing the genre at the same time as doing it. Helped a lot by the girl he sits down with at the end on the bench. It mitigates any 'not being together' feeling that you may have.

With romantic comedy, writers often underestimate the thinking that goes underneath it. The story holding it all up has to be solid. Beyond just a guy and a girl, what's the set-up, what's the obstacle? It doesn't have to be an earth-shattering premise but it has to give the movie a fresh and concrete foundation.

DM: TV is more suitable for exploring the dynamics of a marriage. For a romantic comedy film that's harder to do because they're not settled. *Hope Springs, Quartet, Late Quartet, Best Exotic Marigold Hotel* are great because they're about older, established couples who generally have more complexity in their relationships. Which appeals to the older audience. They don't ignore them.

CASE STUDY: *BRAVE*

In soro/famcom *Brave*, Merida is a very new kind of Disney princess as the object of her obsessions is... her mother, Queen Elinor! The only hint of a wedding is the one that wild Merida absolutely refuses to have, much to the anger of rigid Elinor. Set in the ancient Scottish Highlands where clans maintain peace through traditional arrangements with each other, Elinor is the controlling and authoritative parent who is determined to force her unruly daughter to marry according to tradition. She represents superego, with all its righteousness, insisting that Elinor will wed the young male suitor who wins the Highland Games. Merida is a feminist – she wants equality, life on her terms, and most importantly to jettison all traditional values as espoused by Elinor. But she's going about it with id-like rage and immaturity, leaving mother and daughter at total loggerheads. More significantly, Merida is truly skilled at archery, and easily beats all the wimpy and useless suitors. The last thing she wants is marriage; what she wants is adventure. The deadlock is not helped by Merida being passively indulged by her father, Fergus, and allowed to do whatever she wants, something that antagonises Elinor. When Merida bargains with a witch to escape her fate, Elinor is turned into a bear, with only days before the spell becomes permanent unless a strange command is fulfilled.

The bear, which symbolises bravery in some cultures, as well as the protective mother, reflects the qualities both mother and daughter need to develop to reach understanding. Merida is feisty, fearless, angry, autonomous and a born fighter. She's not defined by traditionally feminine gender traits such as dependency, care for others, subservience, the need for a relationship or the tendency to put herself second. On the surface she is brave, but she needs to learn the bravery of compassion and protection for her mother. Elinor needs to learn tolerance and acceptance, as well as protect and value her daughter's independent spirit.

Both mother and daughter are in fact as tough, raging, un-compromising and determined as each other. Their journey is to learn to appreciate the other, and to show and give to each other consideration, compassion, care, protection and nurture. Fundamentally, they put down their superego defence mechanisms of righteousness to see the other person. In this way the story is a rites of passage for both young and older woman. This doesn't mean that either character will become more traditionally 'feminine', squealing over the colour of bridesmaids' dresses any time soon (although they do make a tapestry together) – rather, that mother and daughter can discover love and respect for one other and heroically defend each other, beyond the clichéd rivalry, resentment and envy that often accompanies fraught mother-daughter relationship stories.

HOT TIPS

- Characters drive stories, so don't underestimate the importance they play. Everything in a romcom comes back to character, so spend time fleshing them out – and then fleshing them out some more.

- Be deep, and then force yourself to be even deeper, when thinking about characters' emotional needs and what it is that prevents them from connecting.

- The protagonist and the significant other don't have to be total opposites. It can be rewarding to explore and discover their deep compatibility. Find out their shared emotional histories, as well as the lessons they stand to teach each other.

- Even though we can easily understand 'typecast' characters, we're always looking for more. Give them unusual hobbies, tastes, attitudes, quirks, etc. to make them feel fresh and original.

- Specificity delivers authenticity, so know as many concrete details about your characters as you can.

- Remember that when characters enter scenes, they've existed elsewhere and have done other things. So through thorough character development, you'll know exactly how your characters should act and react.

LOVE **LESSONS**

Hopefully by now you've got a strong sense of who your characters are and some of the ways they see themselves and cope with life, as well as their deeper needs in terms of relationships. Perhaps you've even applied some psychoanalysis to their development, particularly in how their unconscious might work when it comes to relationships. Now your challenge is to shape and refine the story that this character or these characters have to lead because it's true to who they are. Remember, in a romcom, *character is love story* in the broadest sense.

We want to share with you here an ideation-based approach to shaping character-driven story and structure in a romcom, classic or otherwise, that'll hopefully inspire your visions and choices. At the heart of many romcom screenplays is a character arc – an emotional journey that the protagonist travels, very often from a need or a lack, to fulfilment. Although the most obvious first thing to consider when developing a film might be its plot, often the most important thing to work on first is its emotional journey. This is because it creates resonance in the audience and the characters, leaving them with a strong feeling about the themes and meaning of the story being told. So our approach essentially seeks to inspire your shaping of the emotional journey that your character will take.

STRUCTURE AND PLOT AS EMOTIONAL JOURNEY

As with any screenplay, one of the most important aspects of the romcom is structure. Structure refers to the architecture of a script – or, how story elements are put into place on the page. Structure doesn't just mean plot – it also means structuring the emotional journey, or the character arc. It's also about structuring experience – making decisions about story design so that an audience will feel the story you want to tell. When you start to structure your romcom it can be very useful to think about the plot as a physical representation of the emotional journey. In short, orchestrate the emotion by plotting the action in relevant and meaningful ways. This will ensure that each time the action moves on, so does the character arc. The physical journey and emotional journey are intertwined, working with and for each other.

In Western culture, our films often have a clear 'through-line', firmly, though not always, establishing what the character wants and needs. Three-act structure has become a strong tradition within Western screenwriting for film, and there's much to gain by learning about this. It should, however, be viewed as a creative, not a rigid, endeavour. Stories and their structures are getting more diffuse, experimental and exciting as advances are made in film, TV and online platforms. And so structure is about finding a form that works for your story, not a formula that has to be fulfilled no matter what. Like architecture, screenwriting can work best when a screenplay is developed from the inside out, starting first with the foundations (theme, character arc), then the skeleton (plot, supporting characters), and then adding the more colourful details later (voice, visual motifs).

In the traditional romantic comedy, the overall dramatic shape is about the chase. The two lovers work like protagonist and antagonist to one other, wanting yet rejecting each other. The dramatic goal of each is to be united with the other, and this often starts as a chase initiated by one side, eventually developing into mutual love. The inciting incident is relative to this goal – so, the two lovers meet and then 'unmeet' (reject one another, perhaps), and from this moment on the chase begins. The main drive of the story is related to the conflict between the two, where they and their worlds collide into, and react against, each other. The majority of the story is then characterised by conflict. Because of the comedic demands of the romcom, conflict provides humour and the audience laughs at the star-crossed lovers, cringing at the situations they see them in. The climax typically comes in the form of a reunion of the lovers, where, after a journey from bad to worse to unbelievable, a final event brings the two together. This can often be a mirroring of the inciting incident.

However, romcom now covers so many sub-genres and hybrids, and can be found on so many platforms other than film, that being governed by previous 'rules of romcom' can feel outmoded and there's a good chance the old rules on structure won't really help if your story isn't the familiar boy/girl meets girl/boy.

The order in which information is given to an audience determines their emotional response to the story – tension, surprise, empathy, anger, hope, etc. At first your romcom might seem to have an obvious shape, but that's only the start of things. The same idea can be told in many ways and for many effects – as with the list of sub-genres given above – so working with structure is a key part of discovering how to best express your story. Designing a finely tuned structure is like playing music, where you pluck at the heartstrings of the audience to create the right emotion.

As well as general plot and specific story beats, story design also includes considerations of visual storytelling (including recurring motifs and settings), world and theme. All of these are interwoven, of course, with theme sitting in the middle. Genre plays an important role in story design more broadly, and in story structure more specifically. This is because aspects such as *dramatic shape*, *dramatic goal*, *inciting incident*, *conflict* and *climax* all have their own audience expectations – and, as such, make demands on the screenwriter.

Deciding to use a recurring object as a motif (a love letter or a dating profile, for example) affects the plot, because you need to find meaningful points at which to use the object. Similarly, deciding on the plot your protagonist undertakes will dictate which settings would not only be credible for your scenes, but would also offer meaning, such as juxtaposition or tension. This is why structure is so important in screenwriting – and, to reiterate, understood in the sense of *structuring experience*.

QUICK **INSIGHT**

Gene Wayne Hart, a screenwriter and filmmaker who also runs a romantic comedy film club in Melbourne, Australia.

Attempted confessions

In 1954, Humphrey Bogart's Linus Larrabee gave a full confession to Sabrina (Audrey Hepburn) of the deception underpinning their courtship – a devious plan to protect the family business. Sabrina leaves him and returns to Paris.

But not all heroes have to show such honour and break off the relationship themselves. Probably your hero is a lying scumbag, pretending to be someone he's not, to win the girl. In the logic of a romantic comedy, this lie will have to be exposed somehow, and the hero will have to do penance for it. But how can your hero get out of this jam with honour?

When someone confesses to a crime after they've been caught, you can never be sure if they're sorry they committed the crime, or sorry they were caught. We want complications and obstacles in our romantic comedies. We want to punish our heroes. But we also want our heroes and heroines to be worthy of love. You can have it both ways with the *attempted confession* scene.

The mark of an honourable romantic hero is that, when everything's going well, he's prepared to risk it all and come clean – the attempted confession. We know the hero's a good guy, he tried to come clean, but the other characters don't know that and they punish him – the hero gets his just desserts, while showing that his heart was in the right place.

The best place for an attempted confession is about ten seconds before the hero is caught.

Let's take *Wedding Crashers* as an example. John is lying through his teeth to woo Claire. And he's succeeding. She's falling in love with him. Very dishonourable, wooing a girl under false pretences. But John knows it's gone too far, and he wants to come clean.

John and Claire are outside on the swing. While John is preparing to confess – the 'there's something I need to tell you' moment – Claire's fiancé is in the house receiving a phone call that exposes John for who he really is. Before John can get his words out, all hell breaks loose in the house, everyone rushes out, John is exposed and the fiancé punches him in the face. This creates something of an emotional paradox – we feel John should be punished for lying, and he is, but we know he was going to come clean, so we feel bad for him for being exposed in such a cruel way.

A variation on this is the *misinterpreted confession*, in which case the hero confesses but is misunderstood. There's a particularly lovely version of this scene in *The Hudsucker Proxy*. Amy tries to explain to the dim-witted Norville that she's not a secretary, but an undercover reporter out to expose him. When she starts, Norville cuts Amy off to tell her that he knows she's not who she says she is – he's been aware for some time that she's not a very good secretary, but he won't tell anyone.

An important follow-up to the attempted confession is the *acceptance of guilt*. In *Wedding Crashers*, once exposed, John tries to explain himself, but seeing the hurt he has caused and knowing he's in the wrong, admits it without reservations when Rachel asks him if it's true. He accepts that he was in the wrong and leaves.

Humphrey Bogarts are few and far between these days. More likely your hero is a lying scumbag and deserves what's coming. So give it to him. Just show us that his heart is in the right place first.

THE ASPIRATIONS, INTERVENTIONS AND OUTCOMES APPROACH

Thinking about the emotional journey that your protagonist will take can be seen in the form of a process where he/she/they have some kind of aspiration of the heart, and it's the pursuit – active or passive, conscious or unconscious – of this that shapes and informs the journey. The aspiration encounters interventions – external and internal – that either help or hinder it, or something in-between. This process will have certain outcomes – some closed, some open, some good, some bad. You can see outcomes in terms of 'resolution' or 'lessons'.

By thinking in terms of an aspiration, as opposed to a 'goal' or a 'need' – or even the well-known heroic quest metaphor of the Hero's Journey – you'll be engaging with the character's conscious and unconscious world more actively in your writing from day one. It also means that you can introduce ambivalence, contradiction and other dynamics to your handling of the character's aspiration. If you embrace this in thinking about your comedic love story, it'll perhaps free up your ideation processes considerably as you'll be rooting yourself in the messy matters of the heart from the outset. Also, aspirations in love come and go, are replaced by new ones, live alongside each other, and clash.

As you get to know your character better, you'll undoubtedly be thinking – what does this person need to actually learn? The kinds of lessons you want them to take away by the end of the screenplay will start forming in your mind, so the next task is to work out – how are they going to learn them? Which situations, factors, people, places – i.e. interventions – are you going to give them?

The important thing is to see this as an emotional approach to story ideas – no rights, no wrongs, no rules and no preconceptions involved. Emotions defy logic, which is what makes them such fun to work with as screenwriters.

Let's have a look at each of these aspects in more detail.

ASPIRATIONS

What you aspire to can be conscious, subconscious or unconscious. If the aspiration is conscious, the capability of the protagonist to actually achieve the romantic goal can go hand in hand with their blindspot! A clichéd example is the ugly or shallow chauvinist who thinks the size of his wallet means he can have the hottest girl. The tougher the blindspot, the harder they fall, like Hal in *Shallow Hal*. Or it can be very heartfelt and within reach. In romcoms, aspirations – depending on the sub-genre or hybrid – tend to boil down to three main categories, and many protagonists fit all three.

YEARNING FOR TOGETHERNESS

Yes, the most obvious! The character in the romcom wants, chases and/or represses the need for love. The conscious or unconscious aspiration, clear to the audience if not to the character, is that having intimacy or commitment with another will make them much happier, even if that seems totally unreachable for the character in terms of the emotional state they're in now. Craving togetherness can also take the form of the loss of a loved one, such as in *P.S. I Love You*, where Holly is paralysed by grief when her Irish partner Gerry dies.

FIGHTING FOR AUTONOMY

The character's independence and achievement is their number one priority. This aspiration finds the character motivated to attach a lot of importance to their right to determine their own life, the right to live how they want, and to have everything on their terms. They're 'selfish' to the extent that their selfhood is very motivating. Clearly, this can reflect good self-esteem, but extreme aspects can also reflect a compulsive desire to keep people at arm's length because sharing and compromise feels threatening for some reason. It can also lead to loneliness.

Fighting for autonomy can take the form of a career, a very clear ambition, wanting to be alone, and commitment-phobia. Take Diane in chumcom *Identity Thief* – she's a reckless, selfish criminal doing whatever she can to get money fast to support compulsive consuming. She's out for herself, big time. Violet in *The Five-Year Engagement* loves fiancé Tom deeply, but she's pretty career-orientated, pursuing an academic life in psychology that evolves as a clear aspiration over the five-year span. This is in stark contrast to Tom, who yearns for togetherness from the start, and this doesn't really waver for him – the relationship comes first.

CRAVING HEALING

The protagonist has clear emotional wounds and some scar tissue that's getting in the way of their emotional life moving forward smoothly. The aspiration is to feel better about themselves and life. Like all aspirations, it can be hopeless and remain conscious or unconscious. Take Annie in romantic sorocom/dramedy *Bridesmaids* – she's craving for togetherness with a user-jerk and a best friend who's about to disappear into marriage. But she's also craving healing from a string of disappointments that probably started early in life with her parents' divorce (only hinted at in the film), a failed cupcake business and poverty. However, romantic dramedies that take a character who's suffering due to the loss of a loved one or a relationship, where the character ends up in a more resolved but still lonely state, are increasing, reflecting a truth that sometimes the happy ending comes from accepting and embracing a single life where emotional support comes from within and/or from a wider group of friends.

INTERVENTIONS

How is your character going to achieve their aspirations? You have to decide how conscious or unconscious they are of their aspiration, because it'll substantially influence the interventions they encounter.

INTERNAL CONFLICTS

Your character's primary problem in achieving their aspirations comes down to their personal set of neuroses or their internalised conflicts. The character who yearns for togetherness may feel deep down that they're too fat, too ugly, too old or too dumb. It's up to you to develop appropriate private fears and paranoias. This is the hardest work of character development (and backstory) because you have to a) decide what's happened to the character to make them have these insecurities, and b) create the form these interior conflicts will take, so that they feel emotionally true to the character. Greed, arrogance, insensitivity, inappropriate loyalty, addiction... the list is endless. The point is, they'll appear as interventions for your character's journey during the course of your story.

THE SIGNIFICANT OTHER/OBJECT OF OBSESSION

How you shape the 'intervention' of the significant other is up to you. Your romcom could be like *Hope Springs*, in which the meet cute has long been forgotten after years of increasingly unhappy marriage. Or *Blue Jasmine*, in which Jasmine turns up on her sister's doorstep practically destitute and needing a home and retreat. The first meeting could be in a romantic flashback, as in *The Five-Year Engagement*. How the protagonist encounters the object of obsession serves as the kick-off to many romcoms, and poses the central question – how are these two going to find love with each other, or find happiness again, together or alone?

The significant other frequently embodies enough different qualities to generally explode, over the course of the journey together, the whole identity of the protagonist. You need to work out, from character development, the shape and form of these 'significant other interventions' in terms of personality, interaction, situations and experiences. What's the central conflict created by the object of obsession, and what does this conflict reveal about the protagonist? Is it to do with emotional wounds – like a rejection the protagonist can't deal with? Is it dependency on a teddy bear because they can't move on, like in *Ted*? Or a lifelong bittersweet friendship arresting both parties' development, like in *Sideways*?

INCOMPATIBLE VALUES

Love at first sight is more often a case of indifference or even repugnance at first sight in the romcom. Spending time together, appreciating each other, developing shared interests and having open communication are very often the results of a long battle campaign lasting the majority of the film between the two main characters. Fights, arguments and vendettas are meat and bones to the steamy broth of a romcom. Conflict isn't only entertaining; it raises many active questions, such as, 'How the hell are they going to end up together?' The overall effect of the struggles between two people conveys to the audience a sense of the couple 'earning' compatibility through acceptance. No pain, no gain – or, more romantically speaking, the yin and yang of a union can be achieved. In marriage guidance counselling, it's a common perception that the couple fighting have more of a chance than the couple that no longer gives a damn. A good example of this is *Intolerable Cruelty*.

FRIENDS

Who are we without friends? What do our friends, or lack of them, say about us and our place in life? Who do we choose as friends, and why? What do they need? Ask your character these kinds of questions and work out how friendships feature in the story. The hooking-up-with-friends scenario in a romcom is very familiar. In dramedies, as we've seen, friendship is often the relationship that is under scrutiny, as in *Frances Ha*, who cannot get over the loss of her best friend. Rivalry, betrayal, bitterness, loyalty, fun and escapism – friends can serve the lot. Friends can also be outgrown, embarrassing reminders of our former selves.

In this age of Facebook, friends take on a rather wide and nebulous form as we and they – people we might not know well at all – share comments about what food we ate today, or how cute our child looks. The lonely guy, who aspires to fight for his autonomy due to commitment-phobia, inadequacy, crippling lack of confidence or any other 'loser' trait, but who craves healing deep down, might fall in love with a blow-up doll, an avatar, a fictional character or similar, as *Lars and the Real Girl*, *Ruby Sparks* and *Her* all depict. The 'real buddies' then take on a real intervention as they try to come to terms with what's happening with their friend, accept the weirdness, and then help them get over it. In this sense, do friends serve as positive, negative or ambiguous interventions to the character's aspirations?

FAMILY

Family womb or family tomb? The family group, or just the odd relative, often features in romcoms, sometimes to indicate why the protagonist is the way they are, but equally often to act as an obstacle to be overcome. The family can have a symbolic energy in heterosexual classic romcoms, as if representing the purpose of love – to unite and create a new family, extending the tribe. Sometimes family is a retreat – somewhere the protagonist can return to, to lick their wounds, only to discover that it's a false retreat. In *Failure to Launch*, Tripp doesn't want independence – he needs an intervention to man up and deal with his permanently regressive state, which prevents him from getting a life and forming relationships.

Ultimately we all have to leave the nest and create our own lives. The nature of family connections and the expectations we have of family members are inevitably defined by the wider culture the characters belong to. Some romcoms are firmly rooted in the world of work, which completely dominates the action as intervention on the aspiration, particularly hybrids like *Salmon Fishing in the Yemen* (fisheries in the desert), *This Means War* (espionage) and *Caramel* (a Lebanese beauty salon).

WORK AND COLLEAGUES

Work – or lack of it – is central to your protagonist's identity. Why have they chosen to do what they do? Is work satisfying to them? How does it support or conflict with the central relationship of the romcom? Does the object of their affection/obsession belong to the working world, or is it threatened by the protagonist's job? Work can be a huge interventionist threat to obtaining love or a better sense of identity in the romcom.

In *The Five-Year Engagement*, the resolution of the couple's problems is seemingly achieved at the end by Violet giving up her academic career to serve gourmet fast food created by her ex-chef husband, out of a truck, causing feminist critics' hackles to rise. He's previously given up his top job to back her career, so there's also a message that a lifelong commitment requires an equal level of compromise in a relationship. In real life, of course, conflicting work demands are often a major cause of break-ups.

RITES OF COMMITMENT

Dates, stag nights, hen parties, births, birthdays, weddings, funerals and even divorces provide frequent interventions in the romcom, reflecting back on the protagonist and how 'ready' they are to accept the responsibility of commitment to another person – or to themselves. The bad date symbolically reflects the work that has to be done by the protagonist in terms of open communication, being honest with themselves and others, trust, and – most fundamentally – the ability to accept being loved.

The guys in romantic bromedy *Wedding Crashers* trash the meaning of commitment by lying and screwing their way through the wedding season, reflecting their need to grow up. If your character's aspiration is yearning for togetherness, but she finds herself always the bridesmaid, never the bride, then work's going to have be done (*27 Dresses* and *Baggage Claim*) to break the pattern. Alternatively, if the character's aspiration is career success, like Ryan in *Up in the*

Air, he's not going to make much time for special celebrations that bring people closer.

LESSONS

What does aspiration plus intervention equate to in the romcom? The answer is life and love lessons. Obviously, as your character has their own unique set of aspirations, the lessons they learn are also going to be unique and 'right' for them – and it's your job to define the most essential lessons that this character must learn. Most often, this is to become a whole functioning person able to love another, or themselves, a whole lot better. He or she will develop increased emotional intelligence, some degree of personal growth, and hopefully an increased capacity to feel happiness, with the ability to give and take loving feelings right on top! If you remember the degree of misery your protagonist feels at the beginning of the romcom, it usually takes a steep learning curve to get them to this better place. Your job is to plan those lessons!

Below are some 'lessons' that you can explore in relation to your character. Remember, depending on your theme and tone the character might actually not be able to go the distance and learn the lesson – despite the numerous interventions you've given them. But for feel-good purposes, to which most romcoms aspire, the vast majority of protagonists bite the bullet and meet the challenges you've set for them. It's sometimes far more effective to give a secondary character the role of being bad emotional student!

SHARING

The most popular lesson in the romcom is where the character learns the ability to share – their life, their heart, their bodies, their thoughts, their money and their time. Being in a relationship requires some degree of letting someone in to occupy central space. This is pretty hard to do in real life, let alone for the romantic comedy character. In famromcom *2 Days in New York*, Mingus has to share his partner Marion with her maddening French relatives. In *Notting Hill*, Anna has to share her private life with William, after being accustomed to masking herself for the press. In *Leap Year*, Anna and Declan have to share their unhappiness with life in order to find their true selves, and then true love with each other.

TRUST

Up there with sharing, trust is an important lesson in the romcom. Trusting another with your emotions, your vulnerabilities and your most private truth is a huge and often seemingly insurmountable lesson for many romcom characters. Learning to verbalise that trust, alongside showing it, takes courage. Again, in *Leap Year* Declan has to trust Anna in order to grieve for his late wife – and once he can do that, he's symbolically reborn and then able to move on.

Fundamental to trust is being able to be genuinely truthful, with yourself and with others. Many romcoms show the ongoing suffering of protagonists who simply can't face the truth – about their own problems, their responsibility for these, and their need to move on.

SELF-ESTEEM

Self-love and self-respect are life-changing lessons in the romcom – and the hardest. Protagonists who finally appreciate and value themselves, like Annie in *Bridesmaids* and Muriel in *Muriel's Wedding*, have a far better chance of getting the guy or the girl, and being happy with them.

BEING ALONE AND LETTING GO

Some characters learn that being alone isn't a terrible thing, in fact, and that it's a small price to pay. At the end of *I Love You Phillip Morris*, Steven faces the consequences of his unbelievable crime spree –

being locked in solitary for multiple life sentences. He'll die alone for wanting love, even if we know that he's not going to give up trying. Brooke and Gary in *The Break-Up* gain real closure without continued rage and resentment for each other. By finally achieving closure in an adult fashion they're finally able to move on with dignity.

COURAGE

Learning to put yourself out there and take risks is a big lesson in the romcom. Having the maturity and bravery to face rejection, to take on responsibility for others, to lose material possessions, to metaphorically walk over coals for the one you love, and to stand up for your rights – in love and in the world – are all great lessons in a protagonist's life.

LIFE ISN'T FAIR

The wise character in the romcom has learnt not to pursue empty goals that they'll never win, or the ones that'll ultimately make them unhappy. There might be some residual regret, but the protagonist will be able to walk away knowing that it just wasn't meant to be. They basically don't want what they can't have. Muriel in *Muriel's Wedding* does this, when she realises that she's been leading such a fake life that she must accept who she is for now without the need for a man – and instead embrace her friendship with Rhonda.

LIVING IN THE MOMENT

The resolved romcom protagonist generally exudes a kind of spiritual inner calm. A plateau of self-acceptance and spirituality has been reached in the character's mind, as if they've gained a window onto the secret of genuine happiness. Tim in *About Time* manages to genuinely live in the moment, to appreciate each day and, most fundamentally, to give all of himself to each and every moment.

FEELING JOY

Romcom protagonists can actually start out as a fairly miserable bunch of people! They chase empty dreams, sabotage relationships, hate themselves, hurt others, are envious, jealous, addicted and screwed up, and generally exude 'loser' in one or several areas of their life. An enormous number have so much emotional baggage that they've forgotten the ability to feel and to immerse themselves in pure unadulterated joy. Remember the Greek peasant in *Mamma Mia!*, dumping her sticks? That's the feeling you want your overburdened protagonist to be able to feel – permission to be happy. Shedding the load, and feeling light in spirit and in heart, is a major achievement for these protagonists. It makes all the interventions a price worth paying!

....

EXERCISE - CREATIVE INTERVENTIONS

Brainstorm all the issues your protagonist has in their life – with themselves, their work, their family and the object of their obsession.

Select the top three problems in order of importance to the character in the time frame of the story.

Try to work out a backstory that would logically and illogically (these are emotions, after all!) justify these difficulties. Ask yourself, 'What's the obvious way to heal these problems?'

Now work out a series of 'interventions' in the story that would test and challenge these problems, and ones that would make them more manageable.

Here's an example:

Issue – Envy of best friend/female boss (Aspiration = Craving Healing)

Cause – Problems with mother/sister rivalry, displaced onto best friend/female boss

Intervention – Best friend gets a better job. Protagonist gets sacked/is ditched by boyfriend. Protagonist meets someone worse off than herself. Protagonist loses friend altogether. Protagonist discovers a talent.

....

QUICK **INSIGHT**

Honourable Intentions
Gene Wayne Hart

I remember a friend saying, after a romantic movie, 'Oh that's never going to last, she'll see through him and go back to her husband.' That's the last thing you want someone to say after you've spent two hours trying to convince them that your hero and heroine belong together!

Hopefully your entire narrative, all the conversations the hero and heroine have had, all the fighting and making up, will prove that they should be together. But one trick you can employ, to make us root for the hero, is the *honourable intentions* scene.

In *There's Something About Mary*, Ted chases his long-lost love Mary. Since he can't stop thinking about Mary, Ted hires private detective Pat Healy to track her down. Healy finds Mary and discovers why Ted is still in love with her – she's beautiful! And he's not the only one – the film is full of Mary's suitors. So how do we know Ted is the right one for Mary?

When Healy reports that Mary is no longer the dream girl Ted's been pining for all these years, Ted's shattered. At this stage it seems that Ted was only interested in rekindling a flame with a beautiful girl who got away. Nothing heroic about that. But the next day, Ted comes back to Healy and says, 'I've been thinking about what you said, and I still want to look her up.' And there it is, the honourable intentions scene. That's the moment we know he's the one for Mary. It doesn't matter if Mary is overweight, in a wheelchair, poverty-stricken or has a bunch of kids to different fathers – he still wants to find her.

Now we know his feelings are real, we desperately want Ted to find out what we already know – that Healy was lying. And when, a couple of scenes later, Ted finds out the truth and decides to go to Miami to win Mary back, we know he's doing it because his heart is in the right place, and not just because Mary's 'still a fox'.

As the film progresses, Ted emerges as a worthy hero full of honourable intentions. He confesses to his deceptions, exposes the other suitors, and even withdraws from the contest to nominate Mary's ex-boyfriend, Brett, as her true love. But it's the much earlier honourable intentions scene that puts us on his side.

Compare this with the film *The Heartbreak Kid*. Eddie has just married the beautiful Lila, only to discover she's not the girl of his dreams. Over the first few days of the honeymoon, Lila proves herself to be a grab bag of annoying traits and disappointments – everything from a massive drug debt to singing along with the radio too loudly.

But Lila's not trying to annoy Eddie, she's just being herself. Her heart's in the right place and we feel for her. She apologises over and over again, always trying to make the relationship work. Eddie, on the other hand, is never honest with Lila. He never reveals his true feelings. All attempts to start afresh come from Lila, while Eddie takes every available opportunity to remain distant and to avoid saying what's on his mind. Even when he's trying to break up with her, he's so equivocal that Lila misinterprets the break-up as an even bigger commitment to the marriage.

Though the film's hilarious, we're never on Eddie's side the way we are on Ted's, and when Eddie finally breaks up with Lila and has a chance with new love Miranda, we can leave the cinema wondering if it'll work out, or if Eddie's doomed to heartbreak.

CASE STUDY: *SILVER LININGS PLAYBOOK*

Silver Linings Playbook is an emotional rollercoaster of a romantic dramedy/famcom, which shows the upward struggle of bipolar sufferer Pat to gain control of his mental stability. Character-driven and unpredictable, with a charismatic cast of characters and set in a diverse Baltimore community, the film gives an intimate yet entertaining study of a man who's painfully in denial about the loss of his wife. Pat's lack of balance seriously jeopardises his future happiness, and he faces numerous 'interventions' on a long journey back to recovery.

ASPIRATIONS

Yearning for Togetherness – For the vast majority of his emotional journey, Pat's controlled by a superego defence mechanism of a total inability to face the fact his wife Nicky has left him – and for good. Pat has been incarcerated in a psychiatric institution after losing all control when he found Nicky having sex with a 'history teacher with tenure' in his shower, as their wedding song *Cherie Amour* was playing. This was a catalyst for a complete breakdown, as Pat, we learn, has coped with undiagnosed bipolar and delusional symptoms for most of his life. Pat's conscious aspiration isn't either a helpful or a truthful one, holding him in a state of arrested emotional development.

Craving Healing – To his family, it's obvious that Pat's still borderline out of control, and that he still needs help. When Tiffany meets him, she mistakenly believes he's better than he is, but is soon disappointed that he's still totally stuck. To the audience, Pat's vulnerability is heart-wrenching and we long to see what form the recovery will take. Pat himself wants to heal, but is going the wrong way about it.

INTERVENTIONS

Interventions in *Silver Linings Playbook* are exactly that – everyone connected to Pat wants to help him get better and so take actions, and create situations that they think will help.

Inner conflict – Not being able to control his delusions or outbursts, particularly those triggered by stress, seriously upsets Pat to the extent that 'the Nicky delusion' can be seen as a coping mechanism that he needs to outgrow. If he can get himself well, he'll prove to both himself and her that he's a better man. The trouble is that this is completely inappropriate. He jogs relentlessly, wearing the 'protection' of a bin liner in order to make himself sweat, which also reflects his low opinion of himself – that which he can't admit – as trash. He refuses medication. 'Excelsior' is an important intervention for Pat, a word he clings to that symbolises the supremacy of positivity that will lead to the silver lining moments he also believes in. The trouble is, his faith and conviction are all totally misplaced.

The restraining order preventing Pat from seeing Nicky is also an intervention imposed by the court, but one that he tries to evade. Pat has to attend therapy with caring Dr Patel, a 'formal' intervention that also challenges and tests Pat's fragile world view and self-delusion.

Significant Other – Tiffany is a damaged woman herself whose husband died on the streets. She carries guilt for his death – he was off to buy her sexy underwear to revive their sex life when he was killed – and this resulted in a sex spree at work, followed by her getting the sack. She's trying to forgive herself. She instantly sees the potential for an equal in Pat – someone who's been to the dark side and acquired an honesty – and she aspires to get close to him.

She's shocked to learn how damaged he still is, and how far he has to go to forget Nicky. Essentially, Tiffany represents a potential soulmate but only if Pat can do the right work on himself and heal. She's brutally honest and confronting, something he hates initially but also needs. She offers to fulfil his obsessional need – to get a letter to Nicky – but only if he becomes her dance partner. It's the dance lessons that bring them together, physically and mentally, and this nurturing and intense process begins to loosen the grip of Pat's delusion.

Friends and Family – Pat's father, Patrizio, a bookie and football fan, suffers from obsessive compulsive disorder, and also has a history of no self-control. His own mental health has influenced Pat's functioning. Father and son both provoke and challenge each other, leading to a huge family fight which serves as a turning point for Pat as he now has no choice but to go back on his medication or return to hospital. Pat's mother, Delores, the 'oak' holding the family together, is the one who actively saves her son from eight months of institutionalisation, only to live on tenterhooks in case a clearly unstable Pat makes her regret her decision.

It's the parents who originally support Tiffany 'ambushing' Pat on his manic jogs to get and stay fit for Nicky. They intervene to help him move on. Danny, another patient and best friend to Pat, intervenes when Pat and Tiffany are rehearsing. By showing Pat how to dance with passion, Danny triggers jealousy and possessiveness towards Tiffany in Pat . Eventually, Patrizio's reckless gambling produces a high-stakes intervention to win back money he's lost. He creates a 'parlay' – a double gamble that the Phillies will win a football game, and that Tiffany and Pat will score five at the dance competition. Pat now has to prove his responsibility to himself and others.

LESSONS

The tone of *Silver Linings Playbook* is predominantly compassionate and feel-good, and the lessons that Pat learns reinforce our faith that love, support, family and community can help an almost unreachable person to get better.

Genuine Emotion – Pat learns that he's able to express genuine and truthful emotions. Without medication, he was too manic to actually learn anything. Back on medication, he's calm enough to begin the journey of healing. He feels many things – his family's love; remorse that he's so difficult; empathy and sympathy for Tiffany; the need to protect her; the desire to be truthful; and, last but not least, love based on care and respect. He can actually see another human being, not his own projected idealised other.

Self-esteem – Pat's self-esteem grows through his commitment to a responsibility to Tiffany, and by sticking to a rigorous dance rehearsal routine. His father also shows genuine love and remorse towards him, for spending more time with Pat's older brother in their childhood. Pat is able to feel loved and accepted by his family. He's also able to forgive himself, his father, and Nicky.

Letting Go – When Pat finally discovers the truth – that a letter he has received via Tiffany from Nicky was actually written by Tiffany, who's been lying to him all along – he's able to finally release himself from the power of his self-delusion. Not only does the letter show how much Tiffany cares for him – because she's written caring and tender words about him – he's also confronted with his own lies. We see him able to see Tiffany for the amazing woman she is – and whom he's fallen in love with. At the dance competition Pat finally sees Nicky, who's brought along by Tiffany's destructive sister, Veronica. He's able to see how far he's come as he no longer desires the woman who obsessed him, but can hold on to and protect his real feelings for Tiffany. He has found the courage to let go and move on.

Feeling Joy – When Pat and Tiffany perform at the competition, they exude sexiness, desire, freedom and true jubilation. The dance celebrates Pat and Tiffany's deep connection and journey to heal each other. After the dance, Tiffany mistakes Pat's whispering to Nicky as a sign she's lost him forever, when really he is telling her (we assume) that he's finally moved on. Pat rushes out to find Tiffany, chasing after her, which is a symbolic reversal of all her jogging ambush 'interventions'. Pat tells her he loves her, and they finally kiss. The final scene with the family shows Pat and Tiffany ensconced in each other's arms as Delores, Patrizio and Danny hang out happily. These scenes of union celebrate the long road Pat has travelled to experience genuine happiness.

HOT TIPS

- Passion and joy make us feel alive. Don't hold back! Reach out to your audience with these feelings and emotions.

- Love stories can be increasingly meandering, so take risks with your structure. Do you want a flashback, or several? Go for it!

- Shaping the relationship love story can be an opportunity for your originality and imagination to shine through. Be bold and daring in the journey you build.

- Twists and turns shouldn't feel like a contrived gimmick (unless genuinely hilarious to you). Ups and downs, back and forward moments, being hot and cold are all part of a truthful emotional journey.

- No pain no gain should be your mantra in working out the right interventions needed to heal your protagonist.

- Think about your own life. Aren't we all most alive when the unexpected hits us in the face? Allow unpredictability!

THE WORLD OF LOVE

Creating a compelling and convincing world is one of the most important elements of screenwriting – and one of the least talked about. Creating a world isn't just about creating believability – it influences all other elements of a screenplay, from story to character to dialogue, and it plays a big part in defining the tone of your work.

A well-chosen and well-crafted romantic comedy world creates specific audience experiences – tone and feeling that the plot and characters can't convey by themselves. The world you create also has its own innate dramatic potential, and can in fact belong to particular characters, helping with your story's point of view. By imposing a new world on your characters, or by bringing new characters into their world, you can create interesting and dramatic challenges that they have to deal with. Imagine, for example, a hot-blooded male being put into a quiet and cerebral world of young female virgins. Or an asexual school mistress type of character into a world of jack-the-lads.

A well-developed world can also bring familiar, clichéd stories to life, making them feel fresh and inspiring and, in some cases, more relevant for contemporary audiences. Examples include *Pretty Woman*, *The Devil Wears Prada* and *My Big Fat Greek Wedding*, each of them re-imaginings of the Cinderella love story. A world therefore means far more than just a location for the story to take place in. It is also about:

- The feel of the story – how does the world affect the tone of what we're seeing?
- Internal logic – how does the world operate?
- The emotional experience of the audience – how is it brought about by the world?
- A vessel for theme and meaning – what stories are able to be told in this world?
- Voicing a script – does the world have its own voice, attitude and perspective?

Paris, Je T'aime is a film about a world – a collection of 18 short films that tell a 'love story' about Paris. The film explores what it's like to live in Paris, amongst all of its beauty, disparity and humour. Because the central theme is love – Paris as the city of love, Paris as a place we love – the complete film can be seen as a love story of sorts, one in which comedic love (the mime acts; the lascivious couple; the vampires) is a strong feature.

BUILDING YOUR ROMANTIC COMEDY WORLD

When developing your story, spend as much time as possible building your world. As we've already highlighted, a compelling and original world can make or break your screenplay – not just in terms of appealing to the right producer or director, but also because it can open up your story to fresh and exciting ideas. Spending time on your world can strengthen your screenplay in ways you might not expect – characters, structure, themes, dialogue, etc. Here, then, we want to outline briefly some of the ways you can build the world of your romantic comedy screenplay.

CASTING YOUR WORLD

When working out which characters you need to tell your story, think carefully about your whole cast and the functions they serve.

Your protagonists, for example, are likely to shift between worlds – literally or metaphorically – so you need to know what these worlds are, and how they're working for the story. What happens when he's transported from a grey world of drudgery into a colourful world of sex? What about if she's working in a world dominated by middle-aged and middle-class men, but dreaming of a world run by young, sexy poets who care about the world and the people in it? It's in these worlds that we find dramatic and comedic potential.

The same principles apply to the antagonist. For example, what kind of world do they want to destroy or control, and how does this fit with their situation and personality? What's in a world that threatens them, literally or metaphorically? Remember to think about supporting characters, too, and what they can bring to or from a story world. Do they bring a different type of comedy to the prevailing type? Do they represent the threat of sexual deviance? Do they provide the emotional truths about the protagonists' inabilities to love – in a comedic way?

Questions you might ask about your cast include:

- Which characters belong in your world?
- Which characters don't belong in your world?
- When characters that don't belong in your world still inhabit it, how do they and other characters react?
- What are the character hierarchies of your world, and how are they maintained?
- What relationships exist between the characters and their world? How does the world affect them on a daily basis?

STRUCTURING YOUR WORLD

This is about finding the specific ways in which your world operates – its internal logic included – and how they might shape the structure you use to tell your story. For example, your world might have rules that affect what characters can and can't do. This will affect your structure because character action will be limited. What if it's a world in which men can't lie? Or a world where dating can only happen with the lovers' parents in tow? You might also decide that your world has a specific past or future. Again, this will affect the structure of your screenplay because it means certain things have already happened or will happen. Has a law governing first dates already passed? Or are politicians lobbying to put a ban on unmarried soldiers?

Questions you might ask about your structure include:

- Does the world have a specific, tangible hold on the plot – things that literally can or can't happen?
- Does the world suggest – or demand – a specific emotional arc? What does your world do to people, and how does it trigger character arcs?
- What's the pace or feel of your world, and how does it play out in the sequences and scenes you write?
- Are actions affected by your world? What do characters feel they can and can't do?
- What different versions of your world exist, and how do they play out through the plot?

VOICING YOUR WORLD

It can be surprising yet really illuminating to consider how dialogue can be influenced by a story world. Voicing the world is about finding ways to verbally represent it. Sometimes there are obvious demands on dialogue, such as technical jargon and words or expressions that belong to a specific environment. A romcom set on a spaceship, for example, might require a specific way of speaking that relates to technology, situation and era. But voicing your world goes beyond this – it's also about finding how the world affects characters' attitudes, perspectives and topics of conversation. For example, how would sex-hungry teenagers talk on a night out? What would romantic dreamers talk to each other about? How would a cheating husband react to an authoritarian hotel receptionist bound by a strict identification policy?

Questions you might ask about the voice of your world include:

- What does your world sound like – does it have a universal voice?
- How might characters' dialogue be infected by the world – attitude, perspective, topics of conversation?
- Does dialogue complement or juxtapose the world?
- Is there a style and pace to character dialogue that reflects what the world is all about?
- Are there competing voices in your world, and how do they go about being heard?

THEMING YOUR WORLD

This is about understanding how the world you're creating either demands that certain themes be explored, or else denies the possibility of this. It's about knowing what stories need to be told in your world, and the meaning an audience might be left with. Genre comes into play strongly here because it often dictates the theme of a story, or at least some type of meaning an audience expects. In a romantic comedy, themes can include overcoming emotionally negative experiences from the past, learning to love yourself, and transcending culture in order to be happy. So, when building your world you should consider carefully how specific themes naturally fit or resist.

Questions you might ask about theme include:

- Does your world demand a type of understanding that translates into an obvious theme?
- Which themes are already prevalent in your world, and which are denied?
- How might theme and meaning be woven into your world through characters, action, visual motifs and dialogue?

WORLD AND PLACE

The physical world, in terms of the places and locations in which you set your action, is as relevant to romantic comedy as a detailed fictional universe is to a science fiction film, or a haunted house, creepy forest or psychopath's torture chamber are to horror. The idea of 'location research' might to some sound technical and dry, but in fact it's an essential and often overlooked process in developing a screenplay – especially a romantic comedy screenplay, which can use specific locations to build connotations of romance, love and comedy.

THE CAPITAL CITY

New York. Paris. Rome. London. Seattle. It's hardly surprising that many classic romantic comedies are set in the most beautiful and diverse capital cities of the world. Steeped in history, with iconic and varied settings for moments or great set pieces, a city offers the writer a diverse choice of locations and arenas. But with diversity comes big production costs, so you might want to 'choose wisely' – depending on your ambitions for your screenplay.

As much as the vistas of Buenos Aires inspire you, they might come at a high and unaffordable price for your low-budget quirky indie. A romantic reunion on Brooklyn Bridge for Miranda and Steve in *Sex and the City* provides a special and symbolic 'meeting point' for a couple committed to rebuilding their relationship, but again this kind of scene is probably out of the grasp of a low-budget indie, even with the capabilities of green screen. If you're determined to create an 'urban' romantic comedy because it's essential to your story and your characters, you'll need to find locations and arenas within that city that offer you symbolic and metaphoric resonance.

CASE STUDY: *BEFORE MIDNIGHT*

Before Midnight is the third film about Celine and Jesse whose love story began in *Before Sunrise* in Vienna, and continued over a decade later with *Before Sunset* in Paris. When we meet up with them again, they are in early middle age, on holiday in Greece. Jesse, now a successful novelist (having written a series of books loosely based on their relationship), has been invited by a Greek author to reside at his magical retreat. At the beginning of the film, Jesse says goodbye at the Greek airport to his son Hank who, having spent his holiday with them, is flying back home to his mother, Jesse's ex-wife. Outside, Celine is waiting, with their own two twin girls in the car asleep. They return to the retreat, driving through the Greek landscape, not stopping to see the ruins that they had promised the girls they would explore on the return journey. The usual banter the couple share that we know so well is still there and all seems well and happy. The sun is shining, the setting is sheer paradise, with a twinkling Mediterranean sea lapping the idyllic coastline. Wives chat as they prepare salad for evening in the kitchen. The men discuss freedom, beauty, writing and inspiration against the spectacular backdrop. Both sexes seem assigned to physical territory. Could there be trouble brewing in paradise?

We see ripples of tension in the dynamics of the reconstituted family. When they speak to Hank, Celine seems to dominate the interaction, something that irritates Jesse. There's a distinct gender imbalance in the domestic tasks, and also barbed gender politics jokes at the meal. Later, Jesse and Celine walk to a hotel, the gift of another couple staying at the retreat, to give them a romantic night away from their roles as parents. It is supposed to be a beautiful hotel in a nice little town. Celine is reticent but there is no way to get out of it.

The walk literally takes them from the domestic environment to the supposedly romantic space of a hotel in a quaint town. Halfway, the couple stop in a tiny shrine and joke about the fact they have never married, something their daughters pester them to do. They encounter a billy goat, a symbol of virility. All seems to be looking up for a good night ahead. The walk is a literal and symbolic journey from domesticity to the place of romantic love. As they walk, their old, 'flirty couple' identity returns.

The playful banter only stops when they get to the 'threshold guardian' of the hotel receptionist. Jesse has to sign an autograph in his book to the front desk staff, and we sense Celine's tension, the romance interrupted by other people respecting Jesse. His books describe their encounters, their sex (if fictionalised), and Celine clearly feels defined as a product of his creativity, an uncomfortable place to be. The hotel room, away from people, is rather bland, but soon the spark is restored by exploring the new environment, not least the huge bed in the middle of the room! They are about to make love when Hank calls. Again, Celine won't let Jesse speak to him. She also makes a veiled dig to Hank about his mother – something Jesse disapproves off. From that point, the discussion soon degenerates into an ugly, no-holds-barred row. Celine rages, full of despair about what she has become, raising his kids, her own dreams never realised. His literary career lets him be a cultural nomad with book tours, while she has been grounded in the Pigalle holding the baby. His art means freedom while her 'sacrifice' grounds her, keeps her stuck. The gender battle, hinted at earlier, is now ferocious. Jesse goads her sarcastically about her supposed disadvantages as a privileged Parisienne. Soon the ex-wife is dragged in, Celine cursing her, and refusing to move to the US where Jesse could spend more time with Hank. Chicago would represent death to her, yet another sacrifice she's made on account of Jesse, while to him it would mean an end to the perpetual guilt he feels being away from his son. It's ugly, their marriage and happiness completely trashed by their mutual abuse and resentments. The passionate space of the room has created the wrong kind of passion. Celine storms out.

Jesse finds Celine alone by the harbour, neutral territory after the bedroom battleground, having a drink, clearly down and on the verge of ending the marriage. He tries to win her round, likening himself to a time traveller. Celine reconnects with him, drawn into his humour, seemingly defeated by her own love of him. The water around them suggests healing, calm and hope, at least for the present moment.

Before Midnight uses place powerfully and simply to explore its rich themes of gender conflicts and resentments, family divisions and separations, the beauty and ugliness of marriage, and the inexorability of death. It's a philosophical film that's set in the land of philosophy – Greece. The rich themes create a very contemporary romantic comedy that cleverly combines the tones of awkwardness and compassion. It uses place to explore the idea that a long relationship is one of many journeys we take individually – one that has as many conflicts as it does sources of happiness.

INDUSTRY PERSPECTIVES

So, you've written a great screenplay. It's got a cracking premise, a fantastic cast of characters, an original world, a brilliant narrative structure, dialogue that crackles and a visual landscape that makes the hairs on the back of your neck stand up. So what next? How does this brilliant piece of work make it to the screen? Here's where the really hard work comes in – trying to 'sell' your screenplay. But what do we mean by 'sell'? The first and most important thing to remember is that there isn't only one way of doing it, and different approaches work for different people and situations.

You might have already sold your screenplay to the producer on the basis of a short outline or treatment. They loved the idea so much that they optioned it, meaning that they paid you a sum of money to hold on to the rights to the project for a period of time – six months, a year, five years, etc. Or, you might have made a pre-sale with a distributor who thinks the idea is so strong that they feel they can easily sell it. They were impressed by the project's creative assets – the idea, the director, the actor (if attached), the soundtrack (if created), and even you, the writer. Or, you might have spent so long writing the screenplay that you know it better than you know your own life, meaning that when you go to pitch it to an agent, producer or director, they feel your passion and commission it straight away. Or, you're someone they'd like to get to know better and are considering working with and/or attaching to another of their projects. Or, you might be using a competition or funding scheme to get your screenplay read, and hoping that some kind of commission will follow.

However you approach trying to sell your screenplay – and you'll probably try many options at once – the key morsel of advice is to keep believing in your work and your ability to write, and don't give up. But that's easy to say. The going can get very tough – piles of rejection letters, face-to-face refusals, negative feedback – but if you want to make it, you have to persevere. And you have to think strategically, turning threats into opportunities and weaknesses into strengths. You need to understand the market and learn the tricks of the trade – if, indeed, there are any – and you need to be prepared to network like crazy. That said, you also have to know what you're talking about.

When trying to sell your screenplay, there are various documents that a buyer (or commissioner) might want to read. These are known as pitching documents or selling documents. Basically, they serve two functions. Firstly, they convey the story. This doesn't just mean letting the reader know what happens – though that's a major part of these documents; it means also giving a sense of the style and tone of the film, which includes the theme (how we should 'read' the story). In other words, they should try to evoke a sense of feeling – as if the reader's experiencing the story as they work through the document. This is where good creative writing skills come in, using language to create the tone of the film. This might include vocabulary, syntax and the layout of words on the page.

Secondly, they should give a sense of the scale and logistics of the project so that the reader can gauge how much the film would cost to make, and what kind of production logistics would be required. This includes high-concept idea or not (will it appeal to the masses?), audience demographic (which might link to genre), cast size, locations and potential tie-ins (product placement, funding body schemes, music, actors, etc.). Although discussions about some of this would happen after someone expresses interest in optioning or commissioning your work, it's useful to try to give some sense of it at an early stage. If you think there's a particular benefit or selling point of your project – such as specific audience appeal or talent already attached – you should definitely write about it.

DEVELOPMENT DOCUMENTS

As you work through the creation of your screenplay, you might want to try working with one or more development documents. They can help you to beat out your idea, find focus, experiment with story design and clarify what type of romcom you're actually writing. Development documents can be really useful for taking a step back from your screenplay and understanding – or trying to work out – what's going on. If you're stuck on something, such as a flawed structure or a two-dimensional character, using a development document can help you find solutions. They can be hard and time-consuming to write, and can take you away from the fun of writing the screenplay – but, if done well, they can really be worth the effort.

TYPES OF DEVELOPMENT DOCUMENT

Development documents and selling documents can overlap – such as the treatment – but here we want to run through those that'll help with the idea itself. Although there are common principles that most film personnel abide by, you'll probably find nuances between different producers, directors, script developers, etc. Some of these can be very minor – such as layout and font – but some can be bigger, such as level of detail and style of language. You might also want to develop a document format that suits you and your work – something perhaps not for sending out, but for your reference. This can include online software programs that help to you plan, visualise and prototype ideas, such as Scrivener, Scenepad, SceneTweet and Slugline, and even added functionalities in more mainstream programs such as Final Draft and Celtx.

You need to know the essence of your screenplay – what it's about and why it should be made into a film – and you need to convey it well. Don't be satisfied with a first attempt – keep honing it so it's perfect. This might involve re-reading or thinking more about your screenplay, so that you capture what it's really about and will appeal to the buyer or commissioner – it may very well be your one and only chance. All of this will ensure you're constantly mining your romcom for more – hopefully better – material and producible potential.

Whichever document or form you want to work with, during the development stage you should aim to sketch out and keep building, in layers, the following:

- **Key structural elements.** What happens in your film? Who meets whom, and how, where and when? What conflict ensues? What comedy? How does the romantic climax relate to the inciting incident?

- **Key themes.** What's the film about? Why should an audience care about it? Does your central theme lend itself to a particular romcom sub-genre? How does the protagonist's arc relate to your core message? Do the comedic conflicts represent your thematic concerns?

- **Style, tone and intended audience.** Who's going to want to watch this? How are they going to experience it? What will it feel like to watch these characters explore love and romance? How funny do you want the situations to be – light-hearted or gross-out?

Here are some of the development documents you might want to work with:

LOGLINE

The first document you're likely to need – though it's actually not a document as such – is a logline. This is a short, sharp summary of all that the film is. It's usually only one sentence, though it can sometimes be two, and, in a snappy, clever and 'salesy' way, it needs to spell out who the protagonist is, the dramatic situation and/or world, what the protagonist's goal is – including their motivation – the main antagonism and the theme. Sometimes, too, the logline conveys a sense of the genre. The logline should give a sense of direction and dimensionality – in other words, not just the plot but also the theme. In other words, both the protagonist's physical and emotional journey. Don't confuse a logline with a tagline or strapline – that's something used specifically for advertising, like you'll see on a film's poster and/or DVD cover, and it's more of a hook than something that captures the story.

Here are some examples of possible loglines:

- *I Love You Phillip Morris* – Based on the true story of conman Steven Jay Russell, family man Steven comes out as a gay man and will let nothing stand in his way, including the law, to be with the love of his life – even if it means risking a life sentence of solitary confinement.

- *Leap Year* – When uptight and wealthy Anna follows her boyfriend to Ireland to propose to him, she finds herself thrown into a less-than-desirable road trip with the less-than-desirable Declan, only to be reminded of the true meaning of life and love.

- *Me and You and Everyone We Know* – Christine, a struggling video artist who has trouble connecting with people, finds herself pursuing divorced father-of-two Richard, and through her developing understanding of relationships is able to produce a piece of video art that somebody wants to exhibit.

SYNOPSIS

An extension of the logline is the synopsis. This is a prose document that summarises the story, usually a page in length. A synopsis can be more neutral and matter-of-fact than longer documents, though I'd always encourage you to add dramatic flavour where you can.

A synopsis might use the logline first – as a title, perhaps – followed usually by three paragraphs. Paragraph one sets up the story and the situation – Act 1; paragraph two develops the story and details the complications/hurdles – Act 2; and paragraph three gives the resolution of the story, with its emotional punctuation mark – Act 3. It's important to hit the key beats of the story here, and not give too much detail about things that are less important, as it's the document that might make or break your potential deal – the 'bite' that makes them want to read more (outline, treatment, etc.).

OUTLINE

A longer and more detailed version of the synopsis is the outline. Still a relatively short document in the grand scheme of things – usually two to three pages – it tells the story in its entirety. It can flesh out the key beats more than the synopsis, and better bring out the intended emotion. Secondary characters might be introduced in the outline, too, helping to map the bigger landscape of the narrative. It's usually written in polished, powerful prose – creative writing! – denoting the relevant feeling and tone of the film. The style of writing in the outline can reflect the writer's voice, which again might link with the feeling and tone of the story.

SEQUENCE OUTLINE

A short document, usually only a couple of pages, that gives a condensed overview of the story, broken down into its key sequences, usually eight. You construct the sequence outline by describing each sequence in a short paragraph, considering the film's beginning, middle and end. You can construct a sequence outline by referring to specific structural models, such as Christopher's Vogler's 'Hero's Journey' or Paul Joseph Gulino's 'Sequence Approach'. The sequence outline gives you a clear sense of key plot points and overall structure.

STEP OUTLINE, ALSO KNOWN AS A SCENE-BY-SCENE

This is a bare bones document that maps out the story in separate units or scenes. It gives brief descriptions of each step of the story – usually only a couple of sentences each – telling in brief its physical and emotional beats. A step outline helps you to see the map of the screenplay and work out its key turning points. Usually written in the same font as a screenplay, complete with scene headings, some screenwriters build their screenplay from the step outline. Another way of mapping the steps of your story is to use index cards. With just a couple of sentences on each card to represent each step, you can shuffle them around to experiment with structure.

TREATMENT

A longer document telling the complete story in polished prose. It's a longer version of the outline, giving much more detail. It's much like a short-story version of the screenplay, in which you can add tone and texture. A treatment can be anything between 5 and 35 pages – sometimes longer – depending on what the writer needs. Written in the present tense, the action plays out on the page. The treatment should be broken down into short, concise paragraphs, and key snatches of dialogue may be included, but only if necessary – a recurring key phrase, for example. A treatment is often one of the most important documents used for selling a feature film because of the detail it goes into. In a way, it's just one step short of reading the screenplay – apart from dialogue and visual texture, it lays out all of the action and emotion.

....

EXERCISE – DATING YOUR IDEA

Choose one of the above documents to use for your romantic comedy. Now write it. And then have a go at another one. Remember with each to try to do the following:

- Capture the key structural elements (what happens?)
- Capture the key themes (what's it about?)
- Capture the imagination of the audience (why should I be interested?)

- Capture the style and tone of the film, and its intended audience (who's going to want to watch it?)

....

THINKING STRATEGICALLY

If you don't have an agent representing your work, or are without many of your own industry contacts, you need to consider how you're going to get your script into the right hands – the producer, director, actor or whoever is interested in romantic comedies and wants to make them. Your script might have the overall result of getting you noticed by more established players who like romantic comedy and are not so much interested in your project, but in you as a writer. The options open to you will depend on the country and region in which you are working, but, most importantly, on the market you've identified for your romantic comedy screenplay.

Depending on the kind of project you're working on, and whether you're looking to sustain a career as a screenwriter or just trying to make films yourself, you need to develop a realistic plan for each project. You need to have an idea for how you're going to turn that product into something that's going to get made, or at least optioned, or work as a great 'calling card' script. It's important to also bear in mind that most screenplays do not get produced, but that your script might help you develop as a writer and find people interested in working with you on other projects.

If you're determined to get it produced, you need to be market savvy and keep on top of things – trends, tastes, movements, productions, competitions, funding schemes, etc. You also have to be forward thinking and prepared to make sacrifices in order to achieve your goals, as producing it yourself might be the most viable route at the end of the day. Sacrifices might manifest themselves in a variety of ways, from working evenings and weekends to get the right pitching documents together, to travelling up and down the country to attend networking events and festivals, to spending money on training that will help you understand laws, policies, grant writing, etc., or to reducing the scale of the story so that it can be shot with a micro-budget.

From writing your screenplay and putting together a range of pitching documents, you should have a strong idea about where your project might sit. This could mean commercially – as in, what's a film production company looking for at the minute and does your screenplay have the potential to hit the spot? – and it could mean creatively – as in, what script development schemes are currently 'recruiting' writers and projects, and does yours have something in it that they're looking for (location, theme, genre, etc.)? Whatever opportunities are out there, it's your job to evaluate them and see, where possible, if you can tailor your project accordingly. Sometimes people are looking for screenplays set in particular worlds. Sometimes they're looking for screenplays in a specific genre. And sometimes they're looking for writers of a particular background, who can tell a certain kind of story related to events, people, themes, cultural contexts, etc. Your screenplay isn't going to fit all of these opportunities, but sometimes it pays to think carefully about how you can package it to at least get past the first hurdle. In this sense, you're not just a screenwriter but also someone who knows the bottom line.

QUICK **INSIGHT**

Interview with Ben Cookson, first-time writer-director of Almost Married.

What was the inspiration behind *Almost Married*?

I wanted to write a script about a character who gets themselves into a situation that has the potential to completely destroy their life, but where they're forced to wait a length of time to discover their fate. I wanted to examine that state of limbo; that waiting for results, that feeling of being completely powerless to control the outcome of events, where effectively nothing happens, but at the same time it's often the most dramatic period. I also wanted to write a drama that explored contemporary relationships – so I certainly never set out to write a comedy.

I suppose the inspiration really comes down to being in my late twenties, which is when I wrote it, and what was going around me. People getting married, saying, 'Right, this is it, this is the relationship for me. I'm done!' It's a massive decision, one that poses a lot of questions. A lot of my friends were getting married so naturally I went on a lot of stag nights, which are pretty much the antithesis of everything you are about to do – the last blow out. You're about to enter into a legally binding contract, to say 'I'm yours now, you're mine', but then you have a stag night which, in a way, celebrates being free and single. Mix that in with all the alpha-male bravado and a load of alcohol and mistakes are often made.

How was the writing/development process?

I'd been writing projects that hadn't got off the ground, scripts for other people, spec scripts often with very little money and other ambitious scripts which would be difficult to make as they'd require significant budgets, so I was getting a little bit sick of working on stuff that would ultimately never get realised. So I set out to write *Tested*, or *Almost Married* as it later became, as a low-budget film that I could direct myself. I'd already developed ambitions to direct myself through working with actors in Paris, which I really enjoyed, and I'd also done a short that I'd written and directed, so *Tested* was consciously developed as a first-time writer-director vehicle.

I would ask myself, literally every ten pages, 'If this was a short film could it be made with the limited means at my disposal, cobbled together by friends in the industry?' And if every ten pages I could answer yes to that question, by 90 to 100 pages I knew I would have a script that stood a fighting chance of actually getting made. I had a number of jobs at the time – working for a film festival, teaching English in Paris and doing other little jobs for cash – so I wrote it in my spare time, and it probably took a little over six months. I got feedback from friends, family and old students from Bournemouth University, people whose opinions I valued. Then I went down to Cannes, not knowing anyone, the total writer cliché with a script in my bag and blagged my way in. Literally you have to pay for last-minute accreditation after proving you work in the industry. You queue up with a load of industry bods and can look like a bit of a dick if you get refused for basically being a nobody, which happened to me!

It took me a few tries to get approved. I think, in the end, the woman at the desk just felt sorry for me. I'd been there a couple of days when I bumped into a producer that I'd lost touch with in a bar (we'd originally met in a bar in London). I told him I'd got this script and he asked me to send it to him after the festival, which I did. He got back to me pretty much straight away and said it was one of the few scripts he'd read in one sitting. I sent it to another producer who really liked it as well but couldn't guarantee that I would direct it, mainly because his production company did bigger-budget projects, and for a first-timer it was going to be difficult selling me because I'd done very little. The first guy (the one in the bar) worked on a lower-budget level and he said, 'Yeah, I'll back you as a writer-director. You're the best person to do this.' So I went with him – life's too short – you've got to grab your chances when you can. I didn't want to give something that I worked so hard on to someone else; I suppose I was just desperate to make a proper start on my career. The producer and I have become close friends and the plan is to do a lot more films together.

How was directing it? What did you learn about the different roles of writing and directing?

So many things. Without wanting to sound like a dick, I think the most important thing I learnt is that I can do it. With my background being based in writing I had to prove to myself and the investors that I was capable of directing the feature by shooting a 15-minute teaser, where we tried out kit, crew, shooting styles, cast, etc. Although we subsequently recast two of the leads it was the strength of this teaser that enabled me to go on to do the feature.

With writing and directing you have to wear two hats. As a writer, I enjoy cutting and tightening things, which you continue to do as a director through rehearsals, right down to the edit, but just in a different way. I'd have to say that one of the best things about being a director is working with actors. I'm not the type of director who gets all excited about a new chip in a camera; for me it's all about the story and performance. The other amazing thing about production is working with amazingly talented crew; it's quite a privileged position to be able to work with HoDs who are massively skilled and more knowledgeable than you'll ever be in their chosen fields.

How was it premiered?

We had a premiere at the Mayfair Hotel in London – a full-on red carpet gala. Following this the film received a limited theatrical release – ten screens or something, which is a drop in the ocean but good because you want your film to have the chance to be seen on the big screen.

How did you use social media?

I'm not a particular fan of social media. I understand that it's become a massive part of the industry and I don't mind other people making the most of it, but I just don't feel comfortable self-promoting – I hate it, in fact. When the film came out this kind of thing was handled by a PR company. They deal with the launch, press junkets and interviews. In the development stage you could set up a FB page, tweeting all the time, 'Oh yeah we've just had a casting today, rehearsals going great...' – I really can't be arsed with that. I'd rather just concentrate on getting the job done. And ultimately, if we had done that, it would have been counterproductive because we'd have been promoting the wrong film! We'd have been talking about a film called *Tested* for two years, which was later changed by our sales agent to *Almost Married*. We'd have looked pretty stupid. I'd rather spend time making sure the film's as good as it can be, not updating statuses all the time.

Did you have any concerns about being labelled as a romcom and/or comedy director?

As I said, I never set out to write a romantic comedy; it just became that. It's not my genre of choice. You put these characters in a situation and a comedy arose out of it. That's the way it happened. Comedy is an antidote to stress, isn't it? It got to a point in the writing process where I had to accept that and would look to push the comedy aspect, but for a long time at the beginning I was always saying, 'I'm writing a drama, I'm writing a drama.' And then, at the end, when a sales agent picked up the film, they changed the title and came up with a generic romcom look to the poster in order to help make international sales. To be honest, I don't even think it's a romantic comedy – the film's about a guy who catches an STD whilst on his stag do – the most romantic thing he does is not have sex with his fiancée because he's paranoid he'll infect her with something! Some of the reviews picked up on this warning, 'This is not a run-of-the-mill feel-good romantic comedy. Be prepared...', which I was quite happy about. Some people like to define romantic comedy as a film you could take your boyfriend or girlfriend to, which I totally think this is! Just maybe not on a first date!

Any advice for first-time writer-directors?

If you're starting out as a writer-director, you first and foremost need to concentrate on your writing. For me, the script is still the most important thing; it has to be good. Then – and I don't really like to say this – I think it helps if you're pragmatic about the industry. If I'd written a big-budget period drama or epic war film, it would have been extremely difficult for a producer to raise the money needed with me attached as a first time writer-director.

But if you have a solid script that can be produced within limited means, you will attract a producer, you will attract cast, and hopefully you will get enough money to make it by whatever means possible.

What's next?

The next one could be classed as a romantic comedy. It could be! But I suppose it could come down to how the sales agent and/or distributor want to position it. And if that means more people see it, then great; my only concern is that with this business mentality approach, it might mean that the film doesn't immediately reach its target audience. Originally, when I wrote *Tested*, we were thinking it would appeal to the indie audience. It's about as independent as you're going to get, making a film without any sales or distribution in place, and the STD subject matter isn't exactly mainstream, but the sales agent packaged it in a way that would help them sell it around the world. And it has. It has sold to most of Europe and America and more territories are to follow. And I'm not sure that would have been the case if it had been this little indie called *Tested*. Buyers go to a film market with a shopping list: I'll take a couple of horrors, three romantic comedies, one action, and that's it. If you ever go to a film market, it *is* a market. They could be selling kitchens or dodgy timeshares!

What are you working on now?

A couple of things; one a romantic-thriller, and another which is based on a true story. The second could arguably be placed in the romantic comedy genre, but it's again quite dark. I'm writing it as a drama but can already see, with the characters and the situation they are in, that a certain amount of comedy will arise. So basically another *Tested*!

FINDING FUNDING

Getting money and finding time to write can be hard. If you can't give up your day job, you'll need to carve out your own resources (time, space, mental freedom) to write. As you get more experienced, you should investigate schemes that are geared towards screenwriters working on feature films. National and regional screen bodies and arts organisations have a duty to develop talent and spend a portion of their budget on screenplay development, which you should investigate and try to tap into where they exist. Although such schemes vary from country to country and even from region to region, they all share the same function – to develop local writing talent and create films that are commercially and culturally successful – and may manifest in one of the following ways:

- **Training** – you might be funded to attend screenplay training courses, development hothouses and masterclasses to help raise the quality of your screenplay or of your writing more generally.

- **Research** – you might be funded to undertake research that'll help you complete a screenplay, such as travelling to interview key people and to visit locations, or accessing archives for primary materials.

- **Networking** – you might be funded to attend a screenwriting festival or conference, or similar networking event, to boost the chances of your screenplay being commissioned and made.

- **Mentoring** – probably the most common type of screenplay development funding, you might be funded to work with a script editor, development executive or producer to generate further – better – drafts of your screenplay, ready to offer to the marketplace.

If you're keen to get your romcom made regardless of production companies and broadcasters, especially if you're a writer-director, you might consider crowdfunding as a way of turning your screenplay into a film. Although it's still a relatively new concept, and people have different views about its validity, it works on the same basis as some of the principles used in traditional film financing – namely, that those with a vested interest in having a film made and putting good stories out there will donate money. Although much crowdfunding is done 'in kind', perhaps from family and friends, some of it is achieved in recognition of things like product placement and credit (associate producer, executive producer) – so not at all dissimilar to traditional film financing.

Like self-publishing, some people see films made through crowdfunding as 'vanity films'. Although it's clear where this view comes from, it's not really true. At the end of the day, it's a legitimate way to get a film made – a film that's been written with passion – and although it's not been funded traditionally, it doesn't mean it's of a lesser quality. Such films are often made for specific reasons, too, such as to showcase the writer and/or director's work, which might lead to other projects – or to prove that a particular type of story can be told effectively, which might then lead the way for similar projects to be made via more traditional means.

Popular crowdfunding organisations include Pozible, Indiegogo, Kickstarter and PleaseFundUs. As with most things these days, it's not good enough to just have a product and an opportunity – you need to have a solid communications strategy, which undoubtedly means using social media. If you've got a great romantic comedy screenplay that you want to get made, and the way of getting it made is through a crowdfunding website, you clearly have to drive traffic to that website. If you want the bucks, you have to get the looks!

For example, you might think about setting up a website for the project, which could easily be a Facebook or Wordpress page – where there's a format and design tools already in place, and you simply have to fill it with relevant content and style. This could be complemented by a Twitter account, which you can use to send out project updates and other related newsfeeds. Once you've captured an audience – a Facebook 'like' that's there to stay, and a Twitter 'follower' who's always going to get your updates – you can start to create a virtual community that will hopefully help you both financially and promotionally, such as telling others about the film project.

Although crowdfunding can open the floodgates to a project being realised, there are also things you need to be careful about. For example, what are the funders getting from the project? What can you promise them – and what can you not? Do you have different levels of funding in place, with associated 'prizes' and credits, and, if so, what happens if you raise more or much less than you anticipated? There are also practical things to consider, such as whose bank account will the money go into – the company's or yours – and who's going to manage the Facebook and Twitter accounts – especially if they attract dozens of hits a day. This is where getting a producer on board really helps. Their role is generally much more concerned with project management – budgets, schedules, contracts, etc. – which, as a creative, you might be glad to have in the mix.

There are many facets to a crowdfunded film that you may or may not want to get involved in. If you do, there are potentially great opportunities for your film to be made, giving you that elusive credit as well as the satisfaction of seeing your idea on the screen. And, of course, there are hundreds of well-respected film festivals around the world that might screen your film, which could lead to other opportunities. If you're definitely interested in this type of venture, Spanner Films has compiled a comprehensive guide to crowdfunding, which you should look up online.

HOT TIPS

- Use development documents to help you through the process of writing a screenplay. Don't think they're just useful for pitching and selling. And spend time on them – they might get you out of tricky situations once you start the screenplay.

- Remember that you need to communicate to readers and possible collaborators why they should care about your story. What are its themes? What lies at the core of your characters?

- When pitching, shorter can be better. Loglines are good for starting a conversation – if you can hook them in with one sentence, they might ask you for more.

- Don't be too protective about your work. Screenplays can only be made through collaboration, so get your work out there and get people's reactions. Don't get caught up in fears of people stealing your work.

- There's no harm in making your film through crowdfunding and other 'non-traditional' methods. The key thing is that your work gets made and gets seen – which could lead to bigger and 'better' things.

CONCLUSION

So, how was it for you? Like Andy in *The 40-Year-Old Virgin*, has the sunshine been let in? Do you think you've now got a better understanding of the genre you're writing in, and how you might approach your screenplay – both in terms of writing and selling? We hope so. We wanted this book to be accessible and inspiring, and to help you – the screenwriter – kick-start your romantic comedy project, or go back to it with fresh eyes.

The thing about a screenplay is that it's built up in layers and is concerned with many things, from ideas to themes to structure to visual storytelling to dialogue. As it progresses and develops, new layers are created as a response to new feedback. There are many books and resources about all of these elements, and so what we wanted to give you here was a specific way into understanding the romantic comedy, and also some insights that you might not get elsewhere. For example, we hope that through our tools, principles and examples we've given you new ways to think about the romcom genre and how it relates to various sub-genres, the world of a romantic comedy, tone and the role of comedy, and some help with development, pitching and selling documents.

Many cultures and societies across the world show a 'need' for romantic comedy – to help understand and laugh at ourselves, and the world we live in. The genre will change and evolve, as we, and many others, have suggested, with the proliferation of hybrids and sub-genres. There'll always be a need for films to make us feel loved and wanted and a little less alone – we're human, after all. The romantic comedy is the genre that conveys the notion that there's hope out there for everyone to connect with someone or something.

As writers ourselves, we know the process of creativity is often complex, private and deeply personal. Even more so when writing about love! So be brave, wear your heart on your sleeve, and be willing to share your most private hopes and dreams and disillusions, even if just through your characters. Ideas are special, but vulnerable, just like new love. So nurture them, and protect them.

Enjoy your romcom journey.

FURTHER READING

BOOKS WITH AN ACADEMIC FOCUS

Abbott, S & Jermyn, D (eds) (2008) *Falling in Love Again: Romantic Comedy in Contemporary Cinema*, London: IB Tauris

Bell, S & Gehring, WD (2002) *Romantic vs Screwball Comedy: Charting the Differences*, Lanham, MD: Scarecrow Press

Benjamin, J (1988) *The Bonds of Love: Psychoanalysis, Feminism and the Problems of Domination*, New York: Random House

Deleyto, C (2011) *The Secret Life of Romantic Comedy*, Manchester: Manchester University Press

Evans, PW & Deleyto, C (1998) *Terms of Endearment: Hollywood Romantic Comedies of the 80s and 90s*, Edinburgh: Edinburgh University Press

Freud, S (2005) *The Unconscious*, London: Penguin Modern Classics

Grant, BK (ed) (2012) *Film Genre Reader* (4th edn), Austin, TX: University of Texas Press

Grindon, L (2011) *The Hollywood Romantic Comedy*, Chichester: Wiley-Blackwell

Grodal, T (1997) *Moving Pictures, A New Theory of Film Genres, Feelings and Cognition*, Oxford: Clarendon Press

Harvey, J (1998) *Romantic Comedy in Hollywood: From Lubitsch to Sturges*, Boston: Da Capo Press

Horton, A & Rapf JE (eds) (2012) *A Companion to Film Comedy*, Chichester: Wiley

McDonald, TJ (2007) *Romantic Comedy: Boy Meets Girl Meets Genre*, London: Wallflower Press

Mortimer, C (2010) *Romantic Comedy*, Abingdon: Routledge

BOOKS WITH A PRACTICAL, INDUSTRY FOCUS

Batty, C & Cain, S (2010) *Media Writing: A Practical Introduction*, Basingstoke: Palgrave Macmillan

Batty, C (2012) *Screenplays: How to Write and Sell Them*, Harpenden: Kamera Books

Duncan, SV (2008) *Genre Screenwriting: How to Write Popular Screenplays That Sell*, New York: Continuum

Giglio, K (2012) *Writing the Comedy Blockbuster: The Inappropriate Goal*, Studio City, CA: Michael Wiese Productions

Gulino, PJ (2004) *Screenwriting: The Sequence Approach*, New York: Continuum

Harper, G (ed) (2012) *Inside Creative Writing: Interviews with Contemporary Writers*, Basingstoke: Palgrave Macmillan

Indick, W (2004) *Psychology for Screenwriters: Building Conflict in Your Script*, Studio City, CA: Michael Wiese Productions

Jacey, H (2010) *The Woman in the Story: Creating Memorable Female Characters*, Studio City, CA: Michael Wiese Productions

Mernit, B (2001) *Writing the Romantic Comedy*, New York: Harper Collins

Misch, D (2013) *The Funny Book*, Milwaukee: Applause Theatre and Cinema Books

Owen, A (ed) (2004) *Story and Character: Interviews with British Screenwriters*, London: Bloomsbury

Scott, KC (ed) (2005) *Screenwriters' Masterclass: Screenwriters Discuss Their Greatest Films*, London: Faber & Faber

Selbo, J (2014) *Film Genre for the Screenwriter*, Abingdon: Routledge

Vogler, C (2007) *The Writer's Journey: Mythic Structure for Writers* (3rd edn), Studio City, CA: Michael Wiese Productions

Waldeback, Z & Batty, C (2012) *The Creative Screenwriter: Exercises to Expand Your Craft*, London: Bloomsbury

Yoneda, KF (2011) *The Script-Selling Game: A Hollywood Insider's Look at Getting Your Script Sold and Produced* (2nd edn), Studio City, CA: Michael Wiese Productions

FILMS REFERENCED

(500) Days of Summer (2009)
2 Days in New York (2012)
2 Days in Paris (2007)
21 & Over (2013)
27 Dresses (2008)
40-Year-Old Virgin, The (2005)
About Time (2013)
Adaptation (2002)
Almost Married (2014)
Along Came Polly (2004)
Amelie (2001)
Annie Hall (1977)
Austenland (2013)
Autumn in New York (2000)
Avatar (2009)
Bad Teacher (2011)
Baggage Claim (2013)
Before Midnight (2013)
Before Sunrise (1995)
Before Sunset (2004)
Best Exotic Marigold Hotel, The (2011)
Blue Jasmine (2013)
Brave (2012)
Break-Up, The (2006)
Bride and Prejudice (2004)
Bridesmaids (2011)
Bridget Jones' Diary (2001)
Bringing Up Baby (1938)
Caramel (2007)
Casino Royale (2006)
Change Up, The (2011)

City Lights (1931)
Confessions of a Shopaholic (2009)
Couples Retreat (2009)
Day I Became a Woman, The (2000)
Departed, The (2006)
Descendants, The (2011)
Die Hard (1988)
Divorce – Italian Style (1961)
Due Date (2010)
Enough Said (2013)
Eternal Sunshine of the Spotless Mind (2004)
Failure to Launch (2006)
Fargo (1996)
Fish Called Wanda, A (1988)
Five-Year Engagement, The (2012)
Flower Girl (2009)
Forgetting Sarah Marshall (2008)
Four Weddings and a Funeral (1994)
Frances Ha (2012)
Goddess (2013)
Hangover, The (2009)
Heartbreak Kid, The (2007)
Heat, The (2013)
Her (2013)
Holiday, The (2006)
Hope Springs (2012)
Hors de Prix (2006)
Hudsucker Proxy, The (1994)
I Do (2012)
I Love You Phillip Morris (2009)
I Love You, Man (2009)
Identity Thief (2013)
In Her Shoes (2005)
Intolerable Cruelty (2003)
Intouchables, The (2011)

It Happened One Night (1934)
It's Complicated (2009)
Jerry Maguire (1996)
Julie & Julia (2009)
Killers (2010)
Kissing Jessica Stein (2001)
Lady Eve, The (1941)
Lars and the Real Girl (2007)
Last Holiday (2006)
Leap Year (2010)
Let the Right One In (2008)
Love Actually (2003)
Me and You and Everyone We Know (2005)
Meet the Parents (2000)
Monster-in-Law (2005)
Moonrise Kingdom (2012)
Moonstruck (1987)
Muriel's Wedding (1994)
My Best Friend's Wedding (1997)
My Big Fat Greek Wedding (2002)
Never on Sunday (1960)
New Year's Eve (2011)
Notting Hill (1999)
Oranges, The (2011)
Other Woman, The (2014)
Philadelphia Story, The (1940)
Pineapple Express (2008)
Populaire (2012)
Pretty Woman (1990)
Proposal, The (2009)
P.S. I Love You (2007)
Quartet (2012)
Queen (2014)
Romantics Anonymous (2010)
Ruby Sparks (2012)

Runaway Bride (1999)
Sabrina (1954)
Salmon Fishing in the Yemen (2011)
Sessions, The (2012)
Sex and the City (2008)
Sex and the City 2 (2010)
Shakespeare in Love (1998)
Shallow Hal (2001)
Shaun of the Dead (2004)
Sideways (2004)
Sleepless in Seattle (1993)
Slumdog Millionaire (2008)
Some Like It Hot (1959)
Something's Gotta Give (2003)
Sweet Home Alabama (2002)
Tanghi Argentini (2006)
Ted (2012)
There's Something About Mary (1998)
This is 40 (2012)
This Means War (2012)
Tombstone (1993)
Under the Tuscan Sun (2003)
Up in the Air (2009)
Valentine's Day (2010)
Vicky Cristina Barcelona (2008)
Violet and Daisy (2011)
Waitress (2007)
Warm Bodies (2013)
Wedding Crashers (2005)
What Happens in Vegas (2008)
What's Your Number? (2011)
When Harry Met Sally (1989)
Y Tu Mamá También (2001)
You've Got Mail (1998)
Young Adult (2011)

INDEX

About Us

In addition to Creative Essentials, Oldcastle Books has a number
of other imprints, including No Exit Press, Kamera Books, Pulp!
The Classics, Pocket Essentials and High Stakes Publishing
> oldcastlebooks.co.uk

Check out the kamera film salon for independent, arthouse and
world cinema **> kamera.co.uk**

For more information, media enquiries and review copies please
contact Frances **> frances@oldcastlebooks.com**